How to Love
YOUR WIFE

Second Edition

John R. Buri, PhD

D1262610

YorkshirePublishing
www.yorkshirepublishing.com
Write Now.

Yorkshire Publishing
3207 South Norwood Avenue
Tulsa, Oklahoma 74135
www.YorkshirePublishing.com
918.394.2665

"How to Love Your Wife is filled with insights for young men looking for their soul mate and young husbands trying to figure out how to be good to the woman they love. In this day when young men and women desperately want to avoid divorce and find lasting love, Dr. John Buri lays down a roadmap."

Maggie Gallagher
President, Institute for Marriage and Public Policy
Nationally Syndicated Columnist
and Author of *The Case for Marriage*

"In *How to Love Your Wife*, John Buri has written a practical and informative guide for those men who want to develop and maintain a positive and healthy marriage relationship. Drawing on his experience, his knowledge of research across a variety of disciplines, and his keen understanding of adult behavior, John Buri has provided men with a map of the realities of married life along with concrete suggestions for attaining the type of loving marriage that most men desire. *How to Love Your Wife* is a must-read for any man who desires a healthy, caring, and life-giving marriage."

Burton F. Nolan, Ph.D.
Professor – Marriage and Family Counseling Specialization
Former Chair, UST Graduate School of Professional Psychology

"One of the greatest challenges of our time is to encourage men to marry for the long haul—for life. But a man needs to learn to build a foundation for a successful marriage so that when the going gets tough, he won't just 'hang in there,' but he will work to develop new romance with the woman he has married. In *How to Love Your Wife*, John Buri explains the steps to success in a practical way that men will immediately grasp. And then, for those who want to dig deeper, he explains the social science research behind each point. The result is a one-of-a-kind 'must read' for any man embarking on, or in the midst of, that potentially greatest of human achievements: a marriage rich in love."

Katherine Kersten
Columnist – *Minneapolis Star Tribune Newspaper*
Former Senior Fellow - Center for the American Experiment

"In *How To Love Your Wife*, John Buri speaks in practical and realistic terms to those men who desire a healthy marriage. As an educator, mentor, husband, and father, he has for years been committed to the development of positive, healthy relationships, and now he has extended this commitment as an author. In *How to Love Your Wife*, John Buri has provided an integration of wisdom, current research findings, and concrete suggestions. It was a pleasure to be able to read this book. I have been counseling and educating married couples for years, and it is my hope that many men will seize the opportunity to improve their marriage by reading this book."

Lauris Prinsen, Psychotherapist
Minnesota Psychological Resources

To the love of my life—my wife, Kathy, whose steadfast love has sustained me, whose respect has inspired me, and who has been so much more than a best friend to me

Acknowledgments

There are many people I would like to acknowledge as this book comes to fruition, but there is no one for whom I have deeper appreciation than my wife, Kathy. Throughout the early mornings and the late evenings working on this book, her encouragement has invigorated me. During those frustrating moments when portions of the book just did not want to come together, her reassurance has buoyed me. And throughout, she has challenged me to embrace this project with zeal, integrity, and empathy. But more than anything else, I want to thank her for standing by me over the years, "for better and for worse, for richer and for poorer, in sickness and in health."

I would also like to thank my six children. I had no idea thirty years ago, when we started on this parenting adventure, just how much they would impact my life. But over the years, they have each left their mark on the man that I have become. I am grateful that they have been supportive of my many endeavors, tolerant of my many foibles, and forgiving of my many mistakes. But most of all, I am grateful that they have so actively and ardently engaged in our life together. And I am thankful for the additions of our daughters-in-law, son-in-law, and grandchildren, who have further enriched my life.

I am grateful to a colleague here in the Psychology Department at the University of St. Thomas, John Tauer, who read an earlier version of the manuscript. His suggestions for clarifications and additions were very helpful. Similarly, I would like to thank Maggie Gallagher, president of the Institute for Marriage and Public Policy. Maggie read the initial manuscript and her comments helped to focus the audience for the book. I have also appreciated the helpful input and assistance from numerous people at Tate Publishing.

The contents of this book are based upon the extensive research, counseling, and writing of numerous colleagues who have spent most of their professional lives in the study of marriage and the family. I am indebted to them for their many years of work in the field. With ingenuity and tenacity, they have sought to understand those variables that enable marriages to thrive as well as those that end up thwarting marital success. Our understanding of what makes marriage work has been transformed by their many lucid, insightful, and bold articulations. In particular, I would like to thank the following (although this by no means entails a complete listing): Donald Baucom at the University of North Carolina; Thomas Bradbury, Andrew Christensen, and Benjamin Karney at UCLA; John Gottman at the University of Washington; Howard Markman and Scott Stanley at the University of Denver; Barry McCarthy at American University in Washington, DC; the late Frank Pittman, a former psychiatrist and family therapist in Atlanta, Georgia, and Priscilla Hunt (Better Marriages), Maggie Russell (National Association for Relationship and Marriage Education—NARME), and Diane Sollee (Smart Marriages), who have tirelessly promoted healthy marriages through their conferences, training workshops, and websites.

I would also like to thank those many other individuals who helped in the development of this book. Through our many discussions of marriage and family topics, some have knowingly contributed to the refinement of the ideas in this book. But many others, unknowingly, have contributed through their willingness to share their experiences. Throughout the book, their identities have been disguised, but the insights they provide have been preserved.

Finally, I would be remiss if I did not express my deep gratitude to the Father, the Son, and the Holy Spirit—the fount of love.

TABLE OF CONTENTS

Introduction

Love Brings Life

Willard Harley[1] is a renowned marriage therapist and author, and he has given us a great analogy for marriage. He has suggested that within every marriage there is a Love Bank. Every day we can make love deposits in our marriage. In fact, every day we have countless opportunities to make such deposits. Unfortunately, as with any bank, we can also make love withdrawals. The goal, obviously, is to have a balance sheet where the deposits far outweigh the withdrawals. This is the goal of *How to Love Your Wife*—to help us, as men, maintain a love balance that is continuously in the black.

Over the years I have been struck by how powerful love is. Couples who manage to maintain a healthy love balance (in their Love Bank) seem to be able to handle whatever it is that life throws at them. Whether it be sickness, a failed business venture, in-law difficulties, financial problems, struggling children (to name just a few). Such couples seem to have a hidden reservoir of strength and resilience. They bounce back knowing that they have a teammate with whom they can weather the storms of life, someone who has their back through thick and thin.

But it is a different story with those couples who allow their Love Bank to become depleted. For such couples, marriage slowly becomes more of a burden than a blessing. What had at one time brought life—as if blowing a fresh breeze into the sales of a ship—now begins to be more of a weight, like an anchor that has been tossed overboard. When the Love Bank balance is in the red, what had been a source of renewed vitality increasingly becomes a drain, and even small struggles begin to loom large, seemingly insurmountable.

Admittedly, none of us men marry with the intent of overdrawing our Love Bank, and yet, as witnessed by the landscape of splintered marriages in this country, this is nevertheless what all too often happens. Furthermore, if you are like most men, you probably have not given a lot of thought to what keeps love alive in a marriage. Nor have you probably considered those things that commonly serve to kill love. In reality, it is the rare man who has ever thought about the fact that love never commits suicide—that the only way love dies is if we kill it.

Therefore this book. We are surrounded by news of unhappy spouses and fractured marriages that have emerged from a failure to keep the love alive. It's enough to discourage people from thinking that a successful marriage is even possible in the first place. Either that or you begin to think that having a successful marriage is like buying a lottery ticket, and you simply hope that you are one of the lucky ones.

But the truth is this: The poisons that threaten to suck the love out of marriage—we know what they are and they can be remedied. Keeping the love alive in your marriage is a realistic aspiration—all you have to do is work at it. In the end, the odds of having a loving, satisfying, and life-giving marriage are actually quite high—if you're willing to make it happen. This is what *How to Love Your Wife* is all about. It is my hope that this book will be a source of fresh insights, inspiration, and strength as you work to make the love professed on your wedding day an ongoing reality in your marriage.

CHAPTER #1

It Takes Two

Popping "The Big Question"

About a year after one of my sons graduated from college, his former roommate, Aaron, came to our home in the Twin Cities to visit. Aaron was a well-built young man who obviously had continued to work out following his football days in college. Aaron and my son had gone through a lot together during those college years—lots of hard work, lots of struggles, and yes, I am sure, lots of fun—and they had been there for each other through it all. I had appreciated the fact that my son had found such a good friend in Aaron during those college years, but that weekend my appreciation deepened as I was able to spend more time with Aaron and to see more clearly his openness and his honesty.

> *My father always used to say that when you die, if you've got five real friends, you've had a great life.*
>
> - Lee Iacocca

During Aaron's stay with us, it came out that he was in a serious dating relationship and he was thinking about asking this young woman to marry him. We talked for a little while about what marriage is like—its joys, some of its struggles and difficulties, the deep satisfactions it can bring, and some of the potential pitfalls.

It was clear that Aaron was looking forward to being a husband and a father and that having a good marriage and family was very important to him. It may surprise some readers that Aaron is not unique in this regard: investigations by University of Michigan researchers revealed that 88% of young men in this country believe that having a good marriage and a healthy family life is an important goal in their lives.[1] This book is for all those men who agree.

Possibly An Even Bigger Question: Is She Special?

In the middle of my conversation with Aaron, I asked him if I could pose a rather large question. Since most of my children's friends have come to understand (or have been forewarned) that I may on occasion ask probing questions, Aaron didn't look at all surprised and without hesitating, he said, "Sure, hit me." And so I asked him if this young woman that he was thinking about marrying was special: "Is she someone so special that you want to tell the whole world about her? Is she a gem—someone that you are so fond of that you will easily be able to sacrifice yourself for her benefit?" Aaron suddenly looked as if I had actually hit him. He was visibly taken aback. It was obvious that he didn't have an answer to that question, and since he was a young man of integrity, he was not going to simply make one up. Aaron left that weekend without giving me an answer.

> *I am convinced that if we as a society work diligently in every other area of life and neglect the family, it would be analogous to straightening deck chairs on the Titanic.*
>
> -Stephen Covey

I suspect that I came across to Aaron as a little odd—"Is she special?"—this is not the sort of thing that someone customarily asks about a prospective fiancée. And I am quite certain that Aaron did not understand the reason for my question. How could he? How could he realize the implications of a man's response to this type of question—the commitment to her which it signifies, the willingness to work at the relationship which it expresses, and the rejection of tempting alternatives which it confirms.[2]

> *A Wedding Toast:*
> *I have known many,*
> *Liked a few,*
> *Loved one—*
> *Here's to you!*
>
> - Paul Dickson

———————————————— *John Buri*

A Telling Response

I have been teaching a psychology of marriage and family class at the university level for over twenty-five years, and it is not unusual for me to ask a young man who is in a serious dating relationship just how fond he is of the woman he is dating. The answers I receive are usually very telling. Some of what is said in response to this question is verbal, but often the most important parts of the response are non-verbal. (Yes, it's true, often it's not what we say but how we say it that matters most.[3])

No disguise can long conceal love where it exists, nor feign it where it is lacking.

-La Rochefoucauld

Sometimes in response to this question, the words, "Yeah, she's special," get spoken, but they don't seem to carry much conviction with them. It's as if the man who is speaking is able to say, "Yeah, I guess so; I suppose she's special," and the words end up coming out with a hollow and somewhat lifeless quality to them. Typically when I hear this type of response, I experience a tinge of sadness, especially if the young man who has responded is unaware of what he has just communicated. In such instances, everyone in the class—at least all those who are able to listen beyond the mere words that are spoken—knows that this young man's love for his girlfriend is lukewarm, at best. But unfortunately, he is unable to hear what he has just articulated so clearly. And I find myself hoping that the woman he is dating can hear what he is saying better than he is able to hear it himself.

Contrary to what the dictionary tells us, pretending is potentially the most serious form of deception because it involves living a lie, rather than merely telling one.

- Harriet Lerner

On the other hand, sometimes a young man will jump at the chance to answer this question. As he speaks, his eyes light up and you can hear the excitement in his voice as he talks about

Love, and a cough, cannot be hid.

-George Herbert

the young woman that he loves. His fondness for her is obvious. She is special, and she clearly holds an important place in his life. It is always delightful for me to hear such a response, for when a young man is able to speak so openly and so positively about the love of his life, I am much more certain that he will put himself into the relationship, that he will decide to invest in their life together through the good times as well as through the bad times.

Proud To Be Married To Her

Well, this past summer my son's former roommate, Aaron, got married, but not to the woman he had been dating. He had confided in me that once he got back home to Chicago after that weekend with us, he could not escape the question I had asked him. He tried to ignore it, he tried to force it out of his mind, but it kept nagging at him. And he slowly came to realize that the young woman he had been planning to marry was not someone that he valued that much after all.

When marrying, one should ask oneself this question: Do you believe that you will be able to converse with this woman into your old age?

-Friedrich Nietzsche

This past winter I had an opportunity to meet the woman Aaron did marry. He strolled over with Kaela beside him and he proudly introduced her to me: "This is Kaela. She is that special woman that you encouraged me to find. I am a very fortunate man to have such a wonderful wife!" As Aaron proudly stood there with Kaela, I got the distinct impression that he wasn't standing there displaying one of his many football awards—it wasn't as if he wanted me to meet his "trophy wife." Rather, he was standing with his friend and companion, someone whom he deeply appreciated in his life, and it was clear that he wanted me to appreciate her as well.

Some Good News And Some Bad News

In subsequent conversations with Aaron, it has become obvious that he has started out his marriage with Kaela with a vision for their life together. He knows that Kaela is special in his eyes and he does not want that special-ness to fade away.

> ॐ
>
> *In marriage do thou be wise:*
> *prefer the person before money,*
> *virtue before beauty,*
> *the mind before the body;*
> *then thou has a wife, a friend, a*
> *companion...*
>
> -William Penn

He knows that Kaela has made his life richer and he does not want that richness to dwindle. He knows that Kaela is a great companion for his journey through life and he does not want that friendship with her to shrivel up.

This book is written for all those men who are looking for the kind of marriage that Aaron and Kaela are envisioning for themselves. No doubt many women will read this book as well, but it is actually written for (and typically to) men.

> ॐ
>
> *Many people today don't want*
> *honest answers, insofar as honest*
> *means unpleasant or disturbing.*
> *They want, instead, a soft answer*
> *that turns away anxiety.*
>
> -Louis Kronenberger

Most of us men really do enter marriage anticipating the kind of life with our wives that Aaron and Kaela are looking forward to. Let me say from the outset that it is possible! The past forty-five years of marriage and family research has revealed a lot of what we men need to do to make it happen in our marriages. The information in this book is based on that research. That is the good news.

The bad news is that what you will find in these pages is frequently not easy. Some of you will read things that you may not want to hear, things that are true, but that you don't want to admit. Some of you will begin to see things in your relationship that you wish weren't there and that you may not want to face. Some of you will find things out about yourself that will be painful to acknowledge (and even more painful to change).

This Book Is Not For Everyone

You should be warned from the outset: this book is not for the faint-hearted. It is not for those who are easily discouraged when a hopeful vision comes face to face with the hard work that is necessary to make that vision a reality. But it is for those who have a capacity for tenacity, courage, and honesty—you will need all three of these virtues if you are going to actually realize your hopes for a loving and life-giving marriage.

When the old guys emphasized "for richer or for poorer, in sickness and in health," they weren't being sentimental; they meant it. A commitment like that takes guts.

-Joseph Sittler

It is not my intent to push this type of marriage onto anyone. Over the years in the marriage and family class that I teach, I have gotten to know a number of young men who are not looking for the kind of closeness and companionship with their partner that will be the primary focus of this book. These men have admitted that they simply aren't interested in the level of commitment to a woman or to marriage that such companionship would require of them. If this is you, if you are one of those men who simply isn't looking for someone about whom you care this much, with whom you wish to share the rest of your life "for better or for worse, for richer or for poorer, in sickness and in health, to love and to cherish," then this book is clearly not for you.

Voltaire thought marriage was the only adventure open to cowards. But Voltaire never married, or he would have known that marriage requires a great deal of courage.

-Hubert Downs

A Sense Of Us

But before you decide to close this book and cast it aside, let me offer you the following thoughts for

The one word above all others that makes marriage successful is "ours."

-Robert Quillen

your consideration. There is a wealth of evidence that a key component of successful marriages is the extent to which a couple experiences a marital bond between them—the extent to which they have a sense of "us" or "we."

For example, when most of us marry, we understand that difficulties in life await us, but we anticipate that in marriage we will not be facing these struggles alone—we are now part of a team and whatever life brings, *we* will face it together. And when most of us marry, we understand that there will also be lots of fun times, and we anticipate that in marriage we will not experience these good times in isolation—we have a partner, someone with whom *we* can appreciate these many good times.

Basically, when we marry, most of us anticipate that we have found a life-long companion and friend, someone with whom we can weather the tough times and enjoy the good times. And the research is clear: those couples who make these marital anticipations a reality in their life together—who develop such a sense of "we-ness"—are much more apt to experience the stable, satisfying, and life-giving marriage that they had hoped for.[4] And essentially that is what this book is about: how to be a "we" with the woman you love.

To get the full value of joy you must have somebody to divide it with.

-Mark Twain

Still Special After All These Years

I mentioned that it is always delightful for me when a young man in class is able to freely express his affection for the woman he is dating. But even more delightful is to hear a man talk with warmth, fondness, and affection about the woman he has married.

If a woman is to find happiness at all in her husband, she is to find it in his appreciation and devotion. If that appreciation and devotion are actual, there is the answer to his happiness as well.

-Dale Carnegie

For such men it is obvious that they are married to someone who is special to them. But even more obvious (as the research in this book reveals) is the fact that they have not taken that special-ness for granted. When I talk with such a man, I know that he has put in considerable time and effort to keep that appreciation for his wife alive and growing. In fact, if the truth be told, I know that such men have not just put in time and effort, but they have also put *themselves* into their marriage.

So I might ask each one of us: Is your wife special in your eyes? Is she someone with whom you want to forge a future together? Is she a gem for whom you will be able to make the sacrifices that a life together will entail? Is she someone for whom you are willing to make the changes in your life that will be necessary if you are to esteem her as the love of your life 20 years after you say "I do"?

I doubt that very many of us have ever thought about it before, but the reality is this: if we do not keep our wives special in our eyes, then the hard work of marriage will quickly become a burden. If we allow that special-ness to diminish, then we will easily tire of the daily grind that will sometimes be asked of us in our marriage, and in the end, we will tire of our wives as well.

Rules To Love By

At this point I need to take a brief detour to explain one of the many differences between men and women that will be discussed in this book.[5] The one that I would like to discuss here derives from differences that go all the way

ॐ

A few strong instincts and a few plain rules suffice us.

-Ralph Waldo Emerson

back to our play experiences as boys and girls while we were growing up.

It is admittedly the rare man who has ever reflected on such things, but research has revealed that the play activities of girls are quite different from those of boys.[6] For girls, play often involves free-flowing, relational activities that are short on explicit rules and long on opportunities to be together and to experience closeness. For boys, however, the focus of games is typically on the competitive aspects of the activities and it is important that there be a set of clearly-articulated rules that will define what is appropriate and what is inappropriate when participating in that activity.

The point here is that we men are accustomed to having a set of rules or guidelines that help us understand the parameters of the activities in which we are engaged. From a very early age, this has been the modus operandi of our experience. And a problem many of us run into within the world of love and marriage is the fact that there are so few rules to which we can turn for clarity and direction.

> *I believe half the unhappiness in life comes from people being afraid to go straight at things.*
>
> -William J. Lock

Therefore, throughout this book you will find explicit rules for a successful, loving, life-giving marriage. One of the things that I have appreciated about men over the years has been the fact that we can be direct with each other. (In fact, subtle often doesn't work.) We don't have to sugar coat things—we can simply say it the way it is. Therefore these rules will typically be stated in direct terms. Based on mounds of empirical evidence and years of experience, this is the way it is. If you want your marriage to thrive, if you are like the majority of Americans for whom a happy marriage is one of their top priorities in life,[7] then these rules are for you.

Rules To Love By

When you married, you selected a woman who was special in your eyes. Special does not mean flawless or the most gifted or even the most beautiful. In fact, it is irrelevant whether any other man has found her to be special. But it is very important that you have.

What man among us, if he had a '67 Mustang convertible or a Mickey Mantle rookie card or a baseball autographed by Babe Ruth, wouldn't do what he could to keep them special?

How much more should we see to it that the specialness of our wives is protected!

ॐ

*"And they lived happily ever after"
is one of the most tragic sentences
in literature. It's tragic because it's
a falsehood. It is a myth that has led
generations to expect something
from marriage that is not possible.*

-Joshua Lievman

Every Marriage Is Defective In Some Way

What I am about to say will likely be difficult for some readers to hear. In fact, some may want to utter vehement protests of "not in our marriage!" But in reality, the comments that follow offer a frequently needed perspective on marital reality. The all-too-common fairy tale vision for marriage—"and they lived happily ever after"—has resulted in the disquietude of many couples as they have come face to face with the fact that their actual marriage is quite a bit more difficult than their envisioned marriage.

I think about marriage like I think about living in my home state of Minnesota. You move into marriage in the springtime, but eventually you experience the Minnesota winter with its cold and darkness. Many of us are tempted to give up and move south at this point, not realizing that maybe we've just hit a rough spot in a good marriage. The problem with giving up, of course, is that our next marriage will enter its own winter at some point. So do we just keep moving on, or do we make our stand--with this person, in this season?

—William Doherty

For virtually all of us married couples, it is only a matter of time before we are confronted by the disparity between our hopes for a special, loving marriage and the reality of our day-to-day lives with the real person we have married. It is the rare person who does not go through a period of disillusionment with his marriage.[8] The reason for this is simple: every marriage ends up being a disappointment in some way.

For each of us, married reality falls short of what we had anticipated: maybe it's not enough communication or too much communication, not enough privacy or too much privacy, not enough sex or too much sex, not enough nice things or too many nice things, not enough emotional expressiveness or too much emotional expressiveness, not enough spending of the money you have or too much spending. Whatever it is, disappointment rears its ugly head in virtually every marriage.

In summarizing the many studies confirming this untoward reality, two social science researchers concluded: "In spite of high hopes that many couples undoubtedly bring to marriage, scholars have found that most spouses fail to maintain the relatively high levels of satisfaction they feel during courtship."[9]

This is not a reason for despair (or worse yet, desertion). This is simply a statement of reality. The important thing in the face of this disillusionment is not the fact that it is there, but rather, what do we decide to do with it.

Doubting Her Special-ness

For some, this disillusionment is taken as an indication that their partner is not all that special after all. As one man, Bill, reasoned with me: "I had been looking forward to the day when Jeanne and I would walk down the aisle and be able to start our wonderful life together. I was told that it would be difficult, but people had told me that about lots of other things in my life as well—high school football, college, my first job after graduation—and I never had to push myself a whole lot in any of those things and they all turned out just fine. So I assumed that my marriage would be the same.

> *We have a picture of the perfect partner, but we marry an imperfect person. Then we have two options: Tear up the picture and accept the person, or tear up the person and accept the picture.*
>
> -J. Grant Howard, Jr

"But what I thought would be a marriage made in heaven has been a big disappointment. It's not that Jeanne is a nasty person or that she is unattractive; it's just that she's not the angel I thought she'd be. So what I've found myself wondering a lot lately is: If she really is all that special, as I once thought, then why is this marriage so tough? Nothing that's meant to be is going to be this much work."

Most Things Take Care Of Themselves— Not Quite!

As Bill and I talked, I tried to help him see that what he was experiencing was not all that unusual, that this type of disappointment is a normal and expected part of virtually every marriage. Unfortunately, Bill was one of those men who had spent much of his life with high hopes, but little diligence.[10] He believed that most things in his life would come his way, but he generally expected this to happen without a whole lot of preparation or disciplined effort on his part.

As a result, Bill would often sound positive in his outlook on life, but this was typically achieved by failing to acknowledge potential pitfalls

> *Words without actions are the assassins of idealism.*
>
> -Herbert Hoover

or significant limitations that stared him in the face. He seldom attacked the struggles in his life, but preferred instead to wait for them to take care of themselves. He seldom put forth the effort to plan for the future, to gather the information necessary to tackle the difficulties that reared up in his life, or to spend time in problem solving when things did not turn out as he had hoped. He simply figured that most things would turn out if he just gave them a little time.

> *I would say that the surest measures of a man's... maturity are the harmony, style, joy, and dignity he creates in his marriage, and the pleasure and inspiration he provides for his spouse. An immature person may achieve great success in a career but never in a marriage.*
>
> -Benjamin Spock

Bill often sounded optimistic, but in actuality he lacked those characteristics that distinguish an optimist from a dreamer. Therefore, it was not very surprising that when faced with the work of re-establishing the special-ness that he and his wife once had, Bill chose to leave her to be with another woman, a woman whom he described as "the one I was truly meant to be with in the first place." It was also not surprising that it was only a matter of time before Bill came to the conclusion that this "love of his life" was also a disappointment.[11] And once again he set out to find his dream marriage rather than roll up his sleeves and do the work necessary to make his dreams a reality with the woman he claimed was special in his life.

Not Only "I Do," But Also "I Will"

If you are the type of man (*unlike* Bill): (a) who believes that much in life is accomplished through sensible and diligent effort, (b) who seldom tackles the challenges in life by the seat of your pants, and (c) who is convinced that in virtually every area of life, the well-prepared person is the most likely to succeed, then this book is for you.

I am repeatedly struck by how capable most of us men are. We go off every day and face a whole host of different circumstances with skill, ingenuity, and energy. Day after day, we meet a myriad of challenges, and we meet them with courage, determination, and adaptability. Hardly a day goes by when we are not asked to prove once again that we are up to the task—that we are capable of doing whatever it takes to get the job done—and more often than not, we are successful.

> ॐ
>
> *The development of a really good marriage is not a natural process. It is an achievement.*
>
> -David & Vera Mace

And it is this same concrete, active, and enterprising tenacity that we need to take with us into our marriages. To a large extent, successful marriages are the result of sensible effort by reasonable people, and it is exactly this sort of proactive approach that will enable us day after day to do those sensible things that will promote the vitality of our marriages. For the happily married man, the marriage vows do not simply entail "I do," but they also encompass "I will"—*I will* put forth the sensible effort my marriage deserves and *I will* be a reasonable person.

With this in mind, periodically throughout the book there will be instances of specific advice—we might call them "how tos." In these "Sensible Effort by Reasonable People" inserts, you will find suggestions for concrete ways in which you can make your marriage happen. These suggestions are not meant to be adopted unthinkingly or to be implemented robotically or to be exercised as mere routines. But rather, they are meant to provide a springboard for the active and creative process of being successfully married.

> ॐ
>
> *Patience and tenacity of purpose are worth more than twice their weight of cleverness.*
>
> -Thomas Henry Huxley

SENSIBLE EFFORT

BY REASONABLE PEOPLE

When was the last time you told your wife she is special to you?
- **Tell her clearly**
- **Tell her often**
    - o **And every day is NOT too often**

When was the last time you told your wife *why* she is special to you?
- **Tell her-and the more specific you can be, the better**
- **Maybe its's**
    - o **Her creativity**
    - o **Her gentleness and kindness**
    - o **Her hard work**
    - o **Her honesty and forthrightness**
    - o **Her loving care for your children**
    - o **Her friendship**

When was the last time you let others know that your wife is special to you?
- **Brag about her**
- **And no wife jokes**

Express appreciation for each other.
Accepting each other makes a stable
marriage. Appreciating each other,
however, makes a sensational marriage.

-Brett Selby

All That Glitters Is Not Gold

Virtually all of us will experience the disillusionment derived from the numerous idiosyncrasies and minor imperfections we drag with us into marriage. This is inevitable; we are human. But sometimes the disappointments of marriage are the result of something much deeper than personal preferences and individual quirks.

> *I've never met a person, I don't care what his condition, in whom I could not see possibilities. I don't care how much a man may consider himself a failure, I believe in him, for he can change the thing that is wrong in his life anytime he is prepared and ready to do it. Whenever he develops the desire, he can take away from his life the thing that is defeating it. The capacity for reformation and change lies within.*
> -Preston Bradley

As a child I was playing one day in a shallow creek and I found some small rocks that glittered in the sunlight. Certain that I had found something valuable, I gathered several of those tiny rocks and took them to a family friend who was a jeweler in the small town where I lived. I am sure that this person was laughing on the inside at my childish stupidity, but I am thankful that he was very kind on the outside as he explained to me that what I had found was not all that special after all. It was "fool's gold." It had some of the outward appearance of gold, but it was nothing more than gravel with a little glitter on the outside of it.

Some individuals end up in relationships with people who are different than they appear to be. And I would like to reiterate here that in saying this, I am not referring to those individual differences and minor flaws that we all take with us into our marriages. But rather, I am referring to

>
> *You cannot help men permanently by doing for them what they could and should do for themselves.*
> -Abraham Lincoln

the stark, day-to-day realities of living with someone for whom destructive behavior patterns are lurking just below the surface—those who are physically or emotionally abusive or who are in the grip of addictive behaviors or who are enmeshed in deep emotional struggles. The problem for such individuals is not that they are void of special-ness, but rather, that they will need help (and sometimes professional help) to realize the special-ness that is buried within them.

Enabling Is Not Love

If this describes your spouse, then your experience is much more severe than the normal disappointment in marriage. If this describes your partner, get help.

Maybe you have been hoping that with enough time or enough patience or enough acceptance, you will be able to turn that glitter into gold, but one of the harsh realities of life is that each of us is capable of changing just one person—ourselves. In saying this, I am not suggesting that there isn't anything you can do to facilitate the change process—there is

೮

It takes two people to have a marriage,
but only one is necessary to change it.
We end up feeling helpless in our marriages
because we can't control our partners.
The truth is that we need only learn to control
ourselves. We need to abandon our attempts
to change our mate and instead focus on ourselves.

-Melvin Kinder & Connell Cowan

often much that we can do. But I am suggesting that oftentimes we need assistance in understanding what is truly helpful to those partners who are fighting their personal demons in an effort to become more healthy human beings.

Rules To Love By

If your marriage has been infested by destructive behavior patterns, character flaws, or dysfunctional emotional struggles, get the help you need. This help might come from a counselor, a pastor, a trusted family member, or a close personal friend. Regardless, get the help you need.

Don't wait until things in your marriage have gotten really ugly. Don't wait until it is convenient. Don't wait until you just can't take it any more. By then, it may be too late. By then, the damage to your marriage may be permanent.

I have seen some magnificent human transformations—people who have come to grips with their apparently overpowering anger or depression or anxiety, individuals who have overcome addictions to alcohol, gambling, food, pornography. But one thing that will inevitably impede the progress of personal growth for such individuals is a partner who refuses to look beyond the glitter, a spouse who responds much like the child who settles for fool's gold.

> *Getting help when you are unable to work things out isn't a sign of weakness; it's a sign of intelligence.*
> -Linda & Charlie Bloom

If you are a person who repeatedly ignores the destructive behaviors of your partner, choosing instead to insist on their special-ness despite concrete evidence to the contrary, then you are likely in need of some help. Overlooking the destructive behaviors of one's spouse does not help in the change process; nor does covering up for them or making excuses for their behavior or compensating for their destructiveness—such enabling is not love. No matter how much it may at times appear to be love, enabling is not.[12]

If we truly love someone, then we will desire what is best for them;

> *Facts do not cease to be simply because they are ignored.*
> -Aldous Huxley

and that love will not allow us to overlook or to enable their destructive behaviors. But oftentimes we will need help as we learn to respond to them in a truly loving way that will help them overcome the destructive demons in their lives.[13]

Reason For Hope

For most of us, however, the marital disillusionment we end up facing is not the result of having entwined our lives with such destructive behaviors. Rather, the disillusionment most of us experience is simply a natural consequence of living out the day-to-day realities of marriage to a real person. (And it behooves most of us men to *frequently* remind ourselves that our wives are also living out the day-to-day realities of marriage to a real person...)

> *To get divorced because love has died is like selling your car because it's run out of gas.*
>
> -Diane Sollee

If you have found that much of the special-ness of your partner (or of your marriage) has been rubbed away over time by the realities of your life together, there is no need to abandon hope for the marriage (or as many unfortunately conclude, to abandon the marriage itself). Such marital disappointment is not a reason for marital despair.

> *New love is the brightest, and long love is the greatest, but revived love is the tenderest thing known on earth.*
>
> -Thomas Hardy

The research findings are clear. If the special-ness was there, if you can remember your early years together with warmth and fondness, then there is much reason for hope. If you can recall with admiration the special place your spouse has had in your life, then the probability is very high (nearly 95%) that with diligence and hard work your love for one another will once again come alive.[14]

Few Americans realize it, but the vast majority of couples who contemplate divorce but instead decide to stay together and to invest themselves more fully in the marriage, find that within a few years the special-ness that they once had with one another is re-captured, often with a depth and a richness far beyond what they had previously experienced. As the authors who presented these research findings put it: "While we tend to talk about bad marriages as if they were permanent things, research suggests that marriage is a dynamic relationship.... How many unhappy couples turn their marriages around? The truth is shocking: 86% of unhappily married people who stick it out find that, five years later, their marriages are happier.... Most say they've become very happy indeed." [15]

One advantage of marriage, it seems to me is that when you fall out of love with each other, it keeps you together until you maybe fall in love again.

-Judith Viorst

Not Just Something I Read In A Book

As I write this book, I obviously approach it as a psychologist who has read hundreds of books and articles on the subject— since I teach a course on marriage, it only makes sense that I would be informed by my colleagues in the field.

The contents of this book have also been influenced by the hundreds of men that I have known over the years. They have been single, married, separated, divorced, widowed, and re-married. Their personal stories have been moving, engaging, enlightening, and at times, disheartening. And together they have provided a collective montage of love and marriage.

But I would be remiss if I did not also mention here the significance of my own marriage in the development of this book. When I was a young man (like so many of the young people with whom I end up discussing such things), I was eager to have a marriage that would be happier and more life-giving than the one in which I was raised. And I found the woman with

There are a lot of marriages today that break up just at the point where they could mature and deepen. We are taught to quit when it hurts. But often, it is the times of pain that produce the most growth in a relationship.

-Madeleine L'Engle

John Buri

whom I wanted to make that marriage happen. Kathy was the best thing that had ever happened to me, and it was with her that I wanted to forge my future. And so, after dating for more than five years, we married and we had one of those fairy tale marriages in which the couple lives happily ever after... not!

Unfortunately, within three years of saying "I do," both Kathy and I were experiencing significant levels of disenchantment—marital bliss had been supplanted by marital disillusionment. And day after day, I found myself wondering: How could this happen? How could the love of my life, someone who had been such a source of vigor and vitality, have now become the cause of so much discouragement? How could we have slipped so far in such a short period of time?

And so three years into our marriage, we found ourselves faced with a decision: Do we pack it in, cut our losses, and go our separate ways? Or do we roll up our sleeves, hunker down

> *All those "and they lived happily ever after" fairy tale endings need to be changed to "and they began the very hard work of making their marriage happy."*
>
> -Linda Miles

for the tough responsibilities of a life together, and make our marriage work? We each decided for the latter, and it was the second-best decision I ever made.

Kathy is my best friend. She has been a tremendous source of love, encouragement, and hope in my life. I cannot imagine living without her (and hopefully I will never have to). A few years ago we celebrated our 30th wedding anniversary and as we were reflecting on the road we had traveled together, I knelt down in the crowded restaurant and asked her if she would do another 30 years with me. She said "yes"!

Is It Worth It?

If you find yourself in a place of disillusionment with your marriage, you may wonder if it is worth it. Is it worth the time, the energy, the investment of self to try to breathe life back into your marriage? The answer, unequivocally, is yes!

I have seen way too many married couples decide to go their separate ways in search of a partner who would provide them the happy marriage they were hoping for. And most of these couples have experienced first hand what two researchers concluded from their 15-year investigation of over two thousand married couples: "Many people who divorce and remarry find that their second marriage is no happier than their first."[16]

I have also seen numerous couples recommit themselves to one another and to their marriage (much as Kathy and I did), and they have experienced an amazing resurgence of the love of their early years together, only this time strengthened by the wisdom of experience. And as the research has clearly confirmed, not only does the love in such marriages energize and enrich the lives of the men and women in them, but there are many other benefits as well. Such married couples are better off financially, they live longer and healthier lives, they experience more frequent and more satisfying sex, and they have greater overall life satisfaction.[17] Is it worth it? Yes!

Firmness of purpose is one of the most necessary sinews of character, and one of the best instruments of success. Without it, efforts are wasted in a maze of inconsistencies.

-Lord Chesterfield

Rules To Love By

Set it firmly in your mind that she is worth it and that your marriage is worth it.

Fan the flames of fondness, admiration, and love that you have had for her.

Do not allow thoughts to the contrary to take root in your mind and set about the task of uprooting all those that have already found a home in your thinking.

Gratitude Journaling

Have you ever been lying in bed late at night, dark all around, and all of a sudden you hear a sound? As you lay in bed, quiet everywhere, you hear another sound, and then another. And the more you focus on the sounds, the more of them you hear, until you are certain that something sinister is afoot. It is only later that you find out that it was just the wind rustling leaves outside the window.

What we focus on expands in our consciousness.[18] This is a steadfast principle of human functioning—what we focus on increases—and this is not true just with strange sounds in the middle of the night. It is also true in our marriages.

When we focus on those things in our marriage that have been a disappointment, then it is the disappointments to which our attention will be drawn. If we spend time thinking about what our spouse has failed to do, or what our spouse lacks, or how our spouse has let us down, or how much our spouse complains, or how we wish our spouse would change, then this is what we will notice—what she hasn't done, hasn't accomplished, hasn't changed, hasn't started, hasn't finished. And it will be more and more difficult to notice all the positive things that she brings to your marriage every day. What we focus on expands in our consciousness.

I have an assignment for you—a journaling assignment. I realize that for most of us men, journaling has not been a frequent activity. Nonetheless, every night for the next couple weeks, I would like you think about your wife and spend five to ten minutes each night writing about all those things that you appreciate about her—maybe it's the sparkle in her eyes, or the fact that she works so hard, or her patience with the kids, or her willingness

In writing his autobiography, G. K. Chesterton wanted to find one sentence that described what life was all about. In that one sentence, he said, "The critical thing is whether we take life for granted or whether we take it with gratitude."

-Christopher Peterson and Martin E. P. Seligman

to help others, or the gentle smile she gives you as you walk in the door after a long day, or the fact that she puts up with a lot being married to you. Write as much detail as you can, focusing on those things about your wife for which you could (and should) be grateful.

Obviously, I am not in a position to actually enforce this assignment. If we were in a classroom context (in which your grade would be dependent on the successful completion of this gratitude journaling), then things might be different. But under the circumstances, all I can realistically do is suggest that this assignment be done. [Can I strongly suggest it?] Take some time each night for the next couple weeks to explicitly express in writing what it is about your spouse and your marriage that you appreciate. Don't focus on the negatives—the disappointments, the frustrations, the irritations, the complaining, the aggravations. Only focus on the positives.

> ❦
>
> *Gratitude unlocks the fullness of life. It turns what we have into enough, and more. It turns denial into acceptance, chaos into order, confusion into clarity. It can turn a meal into a feast, a house into a home, a stranger into a friend.*
> *-Melody Beattie*

An attitude of gratitude is not one of those personal dispositions where either you have it or else you don't. Rather, it is a quality that can be cultivated. When we engage in a regular exercise of gratitude—when we consistently and explicitly focus on those things we appreciate rather than on those things about which we are disgruntled—gratitude will begin to grow. Quite literally, we begin to reap what we sow.

For some of us, the special-ness of our wives is still intact. Keep it that way. Practice gratitude. Continue to focus on the positives. But for others of us, that special-ness has been worn away. Through a variety of circumstances and a myriad of life's situations, it has been eroded. If this is you, take the steps necessary to restore that special-ness. Explicitly exercise gratitude—and I can assure you, gratitude journaling is one way that works.[19] Intentionally focus on all the ways in which your wife enriches your life. Deliberately think about those things you appreciate about her, rather than allowing your mind to wander to your disappointments. That special-ness can be restored, and gratitude is the key.

Settling For Less

Unfortunately, for some couples facing disillusionment in the early years of their marriage, trying to restore any special-ness that was there at the start just feels like too much work. It just doesn't seem like there is enough return on the investment of time and energy necessary to make it happen. For some such couples, their response to this perceived reality is less obvious than the overt abandonment of the marriage, but in the long run its effects can be just as destructive to the life-giving potential of a loving marriage.

Either do not attempt at all, or go through with it.

-Ovid

For some individuals, when they come face to face with the disappointments of married life, they decide that the effort necessary to make their realistic hopes for marriage happen just do not seem worth it. They end up settling for something much less than they had originally en-visioned. For the sake of ease, they settle for a vision of their marriage that will not be so difficult to achieve, one that will not require so much of them.

Women maintain and nurture relationships, but men decide if and when they improve.

-Steven Stosny

While it is accurate to say that both husbands and wives can decide to "settle for less" in their marriages, the truth is that this type of response to marital disappointment is far more common for men. Compared with our wives, we are far more likely to lessen our expectations for married life, provided of course that these lowered expecta-tions will also allow us to put less of ourselves into the mar-riage. It is not always the case, but more often than not,

It takes two to make a marriage a success and only one to make it a failure.

-Herbert Samuel

women are seen as the marital experts—it is our wives who end up with much of the responsibility for "making marriage happen"[20]—and most of us don't mind letting them take that responsibility…. as long as it means less work for us.

Obviously this is a rotten way to treat any individual with whom we have entered a partnership. Two-person cooperative ventures, if success is to be realized, require both individuals to invest heavily in that partnership. But what we are talking about here is not just any ordinary two-party cooperative venture—we are talking about our life together with that woman who is the love of our lives. Can you imagine playing in a doubles tennis match with a partner who has decided to let you handle everything your opponents hit except for those shots that he is forced to deal with? Failure would be all but inevitable, and the same is true in our marriages. If we have found someone special and we want to keep her that way, then we cannot settle for less as we live out that love for her.

> ☙
> *Nothing of worth or weight can be achieved with half a mind, with a faint heart, and with a lame endeavor.*
> -Isaac Baron

Tough Decisions, Not Just Once, But Many Times

When I am talking with a man who has begun to give his relationship with the woman he loves little more than "pocket change" from his storehouse of personal resources, we inevitably end up talking about those things that he has really wanted in his life, those things that he has really devoted himself to, those things that he has gone after with real determination. With some men, such a discussion ends up focusing on athletics, for other men, their careers. But in either case, it quickly becomes obvious that they have been able to accom-

> ☙
> *Marriage doesn't just happen! It takes a solid set of decisions, a huge amount of skill, and enormous willpower.*
> -Neil Clark Warren

plish very little of note without a considerable expenditure of time, effort, and energy. The same is true in our marriages!

I was a high school varsity basketball coach for nearly twenty years (my hobby), and at the end of each season, the assistant coaches and I would sit down with the young men who would be returning the next year. We would meet with each of them and talk about their vision for themselves as well as for the team for the coming year, and we would discuss what they would need to do in order to realize that vision.

Each of them walked away from those meetings with a difficult task ahead of them. It takes a tremendous amount of effort to realize one's athletic vision. When the realistic hopes for athletic development come face to face with the hard work necessary to realize those hopes, some tough decisions have to be made, not just once, but many times.

> Marriage has a great deal to offer, but it is not a Magic Kingdom where the usual principles don't apply and where you get something for nothing.
>
> -David & Vera Mace

The same is true in our marriages. When we walk away from our wedding day, we have a difficult task ahead of us. When the realistic hopes for married life come face to face with the hard work necessary to realize those hopes, some tough decisions have to be made, not just once, but many times.

What a well-known college basketball coach had to say about wanting to win might also be applied to marriage.[21] The following is an expanded paraphrase of his comments. It is not the desire to have a loving marriage that matters. Lots of people want that. What is far more important is the willingness to put in the time and the effort and the energy to make that love happen.

Marriages in this country are not perishing for want of well-intentioned men and women—we have plenty of good intentions. But rather, marriages are perishing for want of the courage, the integrity, and the determination that is necessary if those intentions are to become anything more than nice thoughts.

Rules To Love By

The types of questions I asked each of our basket-ball players as we end our meeting I might also ask in the present context.

Are you willing to put forth the time, the effort, and the energy necessary to realize that loving marriage you have envisioned?

Are you willing to do what it will take to keep the love of your life special in your eyes?

How badly do you really want to be able to describe yourself as "deeply in love" with your wife 15 years from now?

CHAPTER #2

Loving The Love Of Your Life

We Marry For Love

Each semester when I teach my psychology of marriage and family course, I will inevitably ask the engaged students in the class why they want to get married. The students who have been put on the spot with this question will initially give me quizzical looks, as if to say: "This is

> ❦
> *At no time in history has so large a proportion of humanity rated love so highly.*
>
> -Morton M. Hunt

some sort of a trick question, right? Isn't it obvious?" And then the explicit response is always the same: "Because we love each other." For the majority of Americans, this is the most reasonable of responses—it seems absurd that anyone would marry for reasons other than love.

But what most of us don't realize (at least those of us who are younger than 70) is that this has not always been the case—people in this country did not always marry for love. In fact, at the start of the 20th century, a more "institutional" form of marriage was the norm. Men and women married primarily for a variety of societal purposes, for example, domestic maintenance, sexual opportunities, bearing and raising children, and providing for the physical well being of family members. However, as we moved into the second half of the 20th century, marriage more and more came to be seen as a place where most of one's needs for love and affection would be met.

It is important here not to lose sight of the fact (as was pointed out in chapter one) that forty-five years of extensive investigation has revealed that there are numerous benefits derived by married couples, as succinctly summarized in the following statement: married men and women "live longer, healthier, happier, sexier, and more affluent lives."[1] But nonetheless, as we forge headlong into the 21st century, it is the rare individual in this country who does not marry for love.[2]

> *There is no greater risk perhaps, than matrimony, but there is nothing happier than a happy marriage..*
>
> -Benjamin Disraeli

Marriage Logic 101

Please allow me to do a quick logic lesson here. If it is true that we marry for love, then the explicit and consistent expression of that love should produce more satisfying and more stable marriages. And the converse should also be true—if we marry for love, then the failure to express that love should have destructive effects upon marriages. As you might suspect, there is considerable research evidence to support this logic. Those couples who regularly and clearly express their affection for one another have more satisfying marriages. And a decline in these experiences of love and affection has repeatedly been cited as a primary reason for failed marriages.[3]

>
> *Loving can cost a lot but not loving always costs more, and those who fail to love often find that want of love is an emptiness that robs joy from life.*
>
> -Merle Shain

Rules To Love By

The bottom line here is obvious. If you want a successful marriage with the love of your life, then express your affection for her, express it clearly and express it often.

Now if you have been following the logic here, an obvious question may be gnawing at your consciousness right now. Let's quickly run through the logic one more time: If we marry for love *and* our marriages are more apt to thrive when that love is expressed *and* our marriages are more apt to falter when that love is not expressed, then the question that is begging for an answer is: Why don't we express our affection for the love of our life more explicitly and more frequently than we do?

> *Love doesn't sit there like a stone, it has to be made, like bread; re-made all the time, made new.*
>
> -Ursula LeGuin

"How Do I Love Thee? Let Me Count The Ways!"

Recently in one of my classes we were discussing the difficulties inherent in long-distance relationships. It is not unusual to find that when two people are in love and they are separated from each other for an extended period of time, their love for one another begins to cool.[4] In the course of this discussion, I talked about how my wife, Kathy, and I had dated during college and how for three years we ended up at schools that were over 100 miles apart. In an effort to squelch the cooling effects of distance on our love for one another, we had agreed to regularly let each other know of our affection. There were no cell phones, e-mailing did not exist, and long distance calls were expensive—so for nearly two years, we sent letters, cards, and care packages to each other *every day*!

At this point, a young man in the class (apparently unaware of the poem by Elizabeth Barrett Browning[5]) remarked: "In how many different ways can you say 'I love you'?" I proceeded to describe the explicit letters of affection (which have long since been hidden from our children); the beating plastic heart with a pair of panties with red hearts on them (the panties wore out long ago, but the heart is still going strong every time I take it out of the box); the teddy bear with open arms with the message: "I wish I was in your arms rather than this bear."

The most prevalent failure of love is the failure to express it.

-Paul E. Johnson

By this time many of the young women in the class were expressing sighs of appreciation. Emanating from many of the young men, however, were audible groans of displeasure. One of these young men even blurted out: "Why do women want to hear so often that we love them? Why isn't it enough to simply let them know it and then leave it at that?"

Some Big Differences

What I encountered in this class is what many couples encounter as they embark on their life's journey with the love of their life: there are some rather large differences between men and women when it comes to relationship sensitivity and expressions of affection.[6] From an early age an important developmental emphasis for girls is to learn to establish close personal relationships, to be sensitive to the ongoing harmony in those relationships, and to express affection (both physical and verbal) in ways that will maintain those relationships. For most of us men, however, it is difficult to imagine us as boys giving much thought to our relationships or spending much time letting our friends know of our affection for them. Instead, our thoughts generally gravitated toward achievement and status, and our activities were typically centered on competition and the accomplishment of goals.[7]

Let me give you a personal example of how these differences can play themselves out. My wife and I have six children, five sons and a daughter. All of them have been very active in sports. When my daughter was a freshman in high school, she made the varsity basketball team. She came home from practice a couple nights before the first game, and as we were eating dinner together and talking about the day, she suddenly burst into tears. Slowly over the next several minutes we learned the reason for her sadness. She was going to be starting in the game that Friday night.

At this point my sons were staring at me with looks of puzzled disbelief. How could she not be overjoyed at her accomplishment? In their minds she had worked hard, she deserved to start, and she should be proud of her achievement. It had never occurred to them to think about how the older players on the team might feel and how this might disrupt the relationships among the girls on the team.

Now it is important here to make it clear that when we are talking about gender differences, we are not talking about dichotomous differences—we are not saying, for example, that men can only be achievement-oriented and women can only be relationship-oriented. Was my daughter incapable of achievement? Obviously not; she was starting on the varsity as a freshman. Were my sons incapable of a relational focus? Not at all; although it was not the first thing that came to their minds, my sons did come to understand and appreciate that their sister was in tears out of concern for some of her teammates.

We Men Are Poorly Prepared

One thing that is blatantly obvious but is seldom sufficiently emphasized is the fact that marriages thrive on expressions of affection. And let's face it—based upon our growing up years, most of us men as we enter marriage find ourselves at a decided disadvantage compared with the woman we love. By the time we enter this domain of a serious loving relationship, she has already had years of experience giving and receiving affection. She has already come to understand that letting someone know that you love them is a natural, ongoing part of any relationship that you value.

The young man in class—the one who asked why women want to hear so often that we love them—didn't understand this. Like most of us, he did not understand that these reasonable expectations of women are the consequence of years of experience with the fact that if you love someone, then you figure out ways to let that person know. So when that special woman in our lives does not receive our affection often enough or clearly enough, it should not surprise us when she begins to wonder just how special she really is in our lives.

Rules To Love By

The fact of the matter is that ongoing meaningful expressions of affection are essential to the vitality of a marriage. This may not have always been the case, but it certainly is in 21st century American culture where the vast majority of people marry for love.

As you consider what is required of you to make your marriage a success, it is crucial that you overtly acknowledge the centrality of regular heartfelt expressions of affection.

Simply stated, most of us men have been poorly prepared for one of the most important factors in a successful, loving marriage—telling the love of our lives clearly, repeatedly, and in a variety of ways that she is special. And to make matters worse, regardless of

Ignorance is bliss.
Not knowing something
is often more comfortable
than knowing it.

-E. D. Hirsch, Jr.

what our developmental deficiencies might be, one huge reality has not changed: marriages flourish when such affection is expressed and they flounder when such affection is not expressed. So what many of us men find ourselves facing is a situation for which we are poorly prepared but a situation that nonetheless demands from us an appropriate response—to love our wives!

Men especially need to communicate.
To tell people years after the fact that they
were the priority is the coward's way.
If men can muster the courage to fire an
employee, tell off a boss, or assume financial
risk, they can dig deep and say the three little
words their wives and children need to hear.

-Fred G. Gosman

SENSIBLE EFFORT

BY REASONABLE PEOPLE

There are many ways to say I love you
- **Some of them are with words**
    - "I love you"
    - "I missed you"
    - "I was looking forward to seeing you after my long day at work"
    - "You are my best friend"
    - "I really enjoy just being with you"
    - "I thought about you many times today, and each time I smiled"
    - "I am growing more and more in love with you every day"
    - "I can't imagine what my life would be like without you"

- **And some of them are word-less**
    - A heartfelt smile
    - Rubbing her shoulders
    - A gentle touch of her hand
    - Massaging her feet
    - Stroking her hair
    - Putting your arm around her
    - A warm embrace when you each come home after a long day

*Married couples who love
each other tell each other a
thousand things without talking.*

-Chinese Proverb

The Three Questions Of Change

What I have come to realize over the years is that when change is required in a person's life (including my own), three questions need to be answered. First, do you *understand* what needs to change? Secondly, are you *capable* of the change? Thirdly, are you *willing* to change? Few of us have likely thought about change in this way before, but it really is this simple. What other alternatives are there? Either we don't get it, or we can't do it, or we're not willing.

Now some of us men may try to argue that we do not understand how to be affectionate or that we are incapable of effective expressions of affection. In fact, in the face of such arguments, I have known women who have purchased whole books for their husbands, hoping that more

> ಠ
> *Once the "what" is decided, the "how" always follows. We must not make the "how" an excuse for not facing and accepting the "what."*
>
> -Pearl Buck

information might be all it would take for these men to once again bring expressions of affection into their marriages.

But if we are honest, most of us men would have to admit that what we need is not more books or more training on how to be affectionate with the women we love. We understand how to be affectionate and we are capable of it—after all, we have done it lots in the past. We have shown the love of our lives over and over again that she is special and that we love her—otherwise she never would have entrusted herself to us in the first place. If we are honest, most of us would have to admit that when it comes to clear and consistent expressions of affection for the woman we love, at the heart of the matter is our willingness.

Conscious Decision? Or Unfocused Oversight?

As I described earlier, when my wife and I were dating I found lots of ways to let her know that I loved her. But once we were married, my displays of affection for Kathy slowly began to decrease. I stopped buying her little surprises to let her know how happy I was that she was in my life and I hardly ever gave her cards with "I love you" messages on them anymore. All those displays of affection had accomplished their goal—she married me! And then, as if it was now time to move on to other accomplishments, I left those displays of affection and I focused on my career goals.

> *Love thrives in the face of all of life's hazards, save one —neglect.*
>
> -John Dryden

I realize that I am not alone here. Our growing up years have trained us well as men. We were taught to focus on the accomplishment of goals, not the maintaining of relationships, and in the middle of a work environment that does not provide raises or promotions for being a loving husband (or a loving father, for that matter), it is easy to lose sight of the priority these expressions of affection once had in our relationship. Admittedly, most of us are still able to make them a priority when there is a concrete goal within reach—we can still be very affectionate when we want sex—but in the ongoing, day-to-day routine of life, it is easy for us to overlook the importance of these displays of affection.

Now don't get me wrong here. In my experience it has not been the case that most of us men have made conscious decisions to stop being affectionate with the love of our lives. I am convinced that it is the rare man who enters marriage thinking: "Once I'm married, then I can let things slide with the woman I love, then I can ease up on this affection thing." Instead, for most of us, it is

> *A successful marriage is an edifice that must be rebuilt every day.*
>
> -Andre Maurois

simply a matter of failing to make the conscious decisions to continue to be affectionate with her. But regardless of whether our failures to love are the result of a conscious decision or an unfocused oversight, the consequences are the same. When our expressions of affection for the love of our lives decrease, then the vitality in our marriages will predictably dwindle.

A Jolt Of Reality

As I mentioned earlier, after my wife and I had been married for a couple years, our relationship began to show the ill effects of my failure to express my love for her. In those quiet moments of truth—when I would silence the demands of graduate school and work, when I would turn off the television, when I would slow down from my athletic pursuits long enough to sit and think—I began to notice that the relationship with the love of my life, which had been so rich and so full, was now day by day growing more stale. And I found myself seriously wondering whether I was actually falling out of love with this woman who had meant the world to me.

Falling in love in easy.
Growing in love must be
worked at with determination.

-Lesley Barfoot

As these wonderings about my marriage began to grow more and more frequent, a jolt of reality hit me one day from an unexpected source. During lunch with a fellow graduate student named Joe, we ended up talking about his marriage to his high school sweetheart and their subsequent divorce. Joe described their early years together this way: "I really loved Joyce. We enjoyed so many activities together and we never seemed to run out of things to talk about. I had never before been that close to anyone. She meant the world to me

I have known men who could
see through the motivations
of others with the skill of a
clairvoyant; only to prove blind
to their own mistakes. I have
been one of these men.

-Bernard M. Baruch

John Buri

and I couldn't imagine my life without her. But after we were married, things changed. It seemed that Joyce didn't enjoy being with me as much. She just didn't seem to love me in the same way anymore."

As Joe talked, my mind began to race as I drew parallels to my own marriage. This conversation seemed to confirm what I had begun to suspect—it was Kathy's fault! She had changed, she had stopped finding ways to connect with me, she had become less loving! As Joe spoke again, his words broke into my private reverie.

> *A single event can awaken within us a stranger totally unknown to us.*
>
> -Antoine de Saint-Exupery

"You know, John," he said, "I recently began to wonder about that. I've begun to wonder if maybe it wasn't me who changed, if it wasn't me who quit investing in the relationship, if it wasn't me who got so goal-driven that I stopped letting Joyce know how important she was in my life. What has triggered these thoughts is that I am now in a serious relationship again, and I've realized that I am giving this new woman in my life the kind of time and attention and affection that I had at one time given to Joyce. I know that it's too late to go back and I know that I will never have an answer to this, but I wonder if I blew it with Joyce. Did I slowly kill our marriage simply because I stopped letting her know how much I loved her?"

Maybe It Was Me?

This conversation with Joe hit me right between the eyes. The woman who had once been the most important thing in my life had become a bother, and I had slowly come to the conclusion that it was her fault, that she was to

> *The man with insight enough to admit his limitations comes nearest to perfection.*
>
> -Johann von Goethe

blame for our failing marriage. But now, in the wake of Joe's articulated reflections, I began to ponder some tough questions.

Was it possible that, like Joe, it was me who was slowly killing my marriage? Could it be that I was taking her for granted? Was I the one who had quit investing in our relationship?

Even though it was over 30 years ago when this was going on in our marriage, I can still vividly remember the internal battle that I experienced. It was so much easier to blame Kathy than to look at how I might be failing in our life together.

I clearly remember wrestling with the temptation that so many married individuals face — to point the finger at my partner. And although I didn't realize it at the time, I now know that it is yielding to this temptation that is the undoing of so many marriages. Once you settle on your partner as the source of the trouble in your marriage, then it is only a small step before you see no reason for change on your part.

We are always willing to fancy ourselves within a little of happiness, and when with repeated efforts we cannot reach it we are willing to persuade ourselves that this happiness is interrupted by an ill-paired mate; if not our mate, then it would be our own fault that it was not achieved.

-Samuel Johnson

As most counselors will tell you, it is much more difficult to work with married couples than with individuals — whenever you work with couples, there is always a readily available scapegoat who can be blamed for whatever problems exist. And most unhappily married couples are more than ready to focus on the imperfections (however small) of their partner, and in the process, overlook their own glaring shortcomings.

Growth begins when we start to admit our own weaknesses.

-Jean Vanier

Rules To Love By

As you reflect on your marriage, don't fall prey to the common pitfalls that are waiting to put a stranglehold on your lasting marital love.

For example, if you fail to take regular stock of your own shortcomings, if you readily find fault with your wife, if you wallow in thoughts that you are not appreciated for all that you do, then you are wandering out into quicksand.

These thoughts will quickly undo the admiration and appreciation for your wife that are the bedrock of a thriving marriage.

The Man In The Mirror

As I personally wrestled with this temptation, trying to avoid that cold, hard, brutally honest look at the man in the mirror, what Joe had told me about his own failed marriage kept reverberating back and forth in my mind. "Maybe *I* was to blame for the dying love in my marriage. Maybe it was largely *my fault* that we were falling out of love."

A man should never be ashamed to own that he has been in the wrong, which is but saying, in other words, that he is wiser today than he was yesterday.

-Jonathan Swift

I did not have any clear answers to these wonderings, but I made a decision nonetheless—I had to find out whether the affection I once had for the love of my life could be revived. How could I simply turn my back and walk away from this woman who had been so special? And therefore I slowly began to once again express affection for Kathy. At first it didn't come easily. This took me by surprise because previously in our relationship it had been so natural and effortless to let her know how much I loved her. But I persisted nonetheless. I kept finding ways to let her know that I loved her. And slowly our marriage once again came alive, slowly we once again began to connect, slowly we once again fell in love.

It sounds very naïve to me now, but (like most men) I had somehow failed to process the fact that if you marry for love, then that is what you should do—you should love your wife! I had somehow failed to understand that if you marry the one you love, then you should let that person know regularly that your love for them is still alive and well.

Now I realize that some readers may not want to agree with this. For example, I know a man, let's call him Pete, who told his wife on their wedding day: "Dear, I'm telling you today that I love you. You probably won't be hearing it a whole lot—I'm just not that kind of guy—but I want you to know that this fact stands until I revoke it."

Honor — a moral cousin of manners — requires your telling the truth about yourself before the wedding.

-Miss Manners

It is certainly true that any one of us is free to choose this approach to expressing affection, but if you do, please inform your partner of this fact *before* your wedding day. Let her know early in the relationship and then she will be free to choose what she would like to do in the light of that reality. (And by the way, as you might suspect, Pete's marriage was not a smashing success—it lasted less than two years.)

Words! Words! I'm so sick of words! I get words all day through. Is that all you blighters can do? Don't talk of stars burning above. If you're in love, show me!

-My Fair Lady

SENSIBLE EFFORT
BY REASONABLE PEOPLE

- Find ways in which you can specifically and concretely let your wife know that you love her
    o A hug
    o A back rub
    o Her favorite ice cream
    o Flowers with a love note
- Go out regularly on date nights
    o To a movie and dinner
    o Dancing
    o For a glass of wine at a patio restaurant
    o And going to your child's soccer game is not a date!
    o Make sure that you don't let other priorities get in the way of these date nights
- Surprise her with small signs of affection
    o A card left on her pillow
    o Flowers delivered to her work
    o A note left on the dashboard
    o An "I love you" written on the bathroom mirror
- Initiate gentle displays of affection
    o Holding hands in church
    o Touching toes while watching TV
    o Looking into her eyes and telling her that you love her
    o Telling her that not only do you love her, but you are in love with her
- Create affectionate moments together
    o Sitting in front of a crackling fire
    o Taking a long, leisurely walk by a lake (or on a lake if you live in Minnesota)
    o Simply laying in bed together on a Saturday morning and then go get a cup of coffee

My Feelings Have Changed

There can be little doubt that marriages thrive on expressions of affection. And most of us could use frequent reminders of this fact. With all of the many other things in our lives vying for our attention—jobs, bills, children, to name a few—it is easy to lose sight of the importance of letting the love of your life know that she is just that. And admittedly, we men generally need a few more reminders of this than do our wives. But for some couples, reminders alone are not sufficient to engender the displays of affection that are necessary to enrich their marriage. For some couples, there is a deeper issue than forgetfulness that impacts their regular expressions of love for one another. A clear case of this issue can be seen in the marriage of Meg and James.

> ❦
> *Nothing proves better*
> *the necessity of an*
> *indissoluble marriage*
> *than the instability of feelings.*
>
> -Honore de Balzac

This couple had met through mutual friends when they were 23, and soon after meeting, they discovered that they had a lot in common and that they enjoyed one another's company. It was only a matter of time before they were dating each other exclusively, and after three years, certain of their love for one another, they married. But now, only four years later, James was questioning his love for Meg: "I know I loved Meg—that's why I married her—but over the last year I've noticed that my feelings for her have been changing. It's not like Meg is unattractive—she's very cute—and it's not that she has let me down in some way. It's just that I don't feel the same way about her that I did."

> ❦
> *Love talked about can*
> *be easily turned aside, but*
> *love demonstrated is irresistible.*
>
> -W. Stanley Mooneyham

How Did I Get To This Point?

As we talked, I commented to James that he had mentioned that it was about a year ago when he began noticing a change in his feelings for Meg, and so I asked him if there had been anything unusual that had taken place around that time. At first he couldn't recall anything specific, but the longer we talked, the more James remembered: "There was something that happened right around that time. We were going through a lot of changes at work and things were really nuts. People were being re-located and lots of people were laid off. I was lucky to keep my job, but there isn't a day that goes by when I don't worry that I might be next. And then there is the work load—those of us who still have a job are really busy. We're each doing the work that three people used to do.

> *There is love, of course.*
> *And then there's life,*
> *its arch-enemy.*
>
> -Jean Anouilh

"As you might suspect, I have been really stressed, and when I get home all I want to do is watch television and try to shut out all the pressure I'm under. The strange thing is that Meg has really been there for me. She has listened to my complaining, she has been understanding, and she hasn't nagged me a lot about the things that need to be done around the house. It just doesn't make sense that I should feel the way I do about Meg. I just can't understand how we got to this point."

But I Haven't Felt Like It

Somehow Meg had gone from being the love of James's life to barely being lovable, and yet there were no objective reasons that could account for these changes. James was obviously (and understandably) confused by the

> *Love doesn't commit suicide.*
> *We have to kill it. It often*
> *simply dies of our neglect.*
>
> -Diane Sollee

fact that his love for Meg was dying, and yet he didn't know how it had gotten that way.

As we continued to talk, I asked James whether he had shown Meg much affection during the past year when things were so stressful at work. James thought about it for a few minutes and then he responded: "To be very honest, about the only time that I have been affectionate is when I have been horny. I knew that if I wasn't affectionate, Meg wouldn't be interested in sex. But most of the time, I have been so preoccupied with the stuff at work and so stressed out that the feelings of affection for Meg have been drowned out. So I guess the straight answer is no, I haven't given Meg a whole lot of affection during the last year. But quite honestly, it doesn't make a whole lot of sense to try to be affectionate when you just don't feel like it."

Love begets love.

-Robert Herrick

The Drowning Out Of Affection

What James and Meg experienced in their relationship has sabotaged millions of marriages. Certainly pressures from the workplace had their effects—numerous studies have suggested the potential negative effects of work stress on American marriages[8]—but the real culprit in the demise of James's and Meg's marriage was not workplace spillover.

I don't want to sound heartless here, and I am not trying to minimize the pressures many of us experience at work—I understand through years of experience (my own as well as that of numerous men I have known) that work stress can be intense and personally stifling. But nonetheless, for the sake of the desire that many of us have for lasting married love, the following has to be said.

Your living is determined not so much by what life brings to you as by the attitude you bring to life; not so much by what happens to you as by the way your mind looks at what happens.

-John Homer Miller

The real culprit in James's and Meg's marriage (just as in many of our own) was not the work pressures themselves, but rather, the place of prominence James gave to the feelings of stress in his life. Simply put, because he was stressed, James "didn't feel like" expressing affection for Meg, and therefore he didn't. And anytime we allow the residue of workplace stress (or any other stress for that matter) to dominate the day-to-day reality of the marriage with the woman we love, then we are predictably headed for marital lethargy.

> ॐ
> *We become just by the practice of just actions, self-controlled by exercising self-control, and courageous by performing acts of courage.*
>
> -Aristotle

It should not be difficult to see how this type of reasoning will inevitably render its destructive consequences on enduring married love. For one person, it's the problem of feeling down: "How can I be affectionate when I am so discouraged and feel so low; once I feel more upbeat, then I'll be more loving toward my spouse." For another person, it's anger: "I just can't be warm and loving when I'm so upset; I have to get over my angry feelings first." For another, it's fatigue and accompanying grumpiness: "I am so exhausted and in such a rotten mood that I just can't be involved and affectionate; maybe once I get a little vacation I'll be more loving." And for a fourth, it's stress: "When I am feeling so overwhelmed, I just can't give affection; once I feel more on top of things, then I can be more loving." And the list goes on.[9]

Just Do It

Given the many different emotional reactions that can interfere with the feelings of affection that we have for the love of our life, is it any wonder that this type of thinking can have such devastating effects on a marriage? As with James, if our feelings of affection are drowned out by other emotions and we refuse to be affectionate with our wives unless those feelings of love return, then it is predictably only a matter of time before our affection for the love of our life will begin to die.

As you might suspect, this type of reasoning—once I feel more loving, then I'll start to act that way, too—has an enticing appeal for many Americans. But what you may not suspect is that this sort of reasoning has been identified as a primary thought pattern that serves to undermine marital love.[10] With the myriad of emotional states that each of us experience on a regular basis (a fair share of them admittedly negative), is it any wonder that this type of thinking is so destructive to married love?

But what may not be nearly so obvious is the fact that literally hundreds of studies have revealed just the opposite. When our emotions tell us one thing and we act contrary to those feelings, then how we feel typically changes in the direction of the behavior we have chosen.[11] Some people may not want to hear it (especially those like James, who believe that they have to feel loving before they can be loving), but one of the best ways to revive the love in your relationship is to be loving. As a noted marriage therapist stated so succinctly: "People feel more loving if they act more loving, and a relationship in which they act loving will certainly make them feel far better about themselves and their partner....Above all, people who want to feel loving should start by acting loving—at home."[12]

> ॐ
> *The emotions are not always subject to reason...but they are always subject to action. When thoughts do not neutralize an undesirable emotion, actions will.*
>
> -William James

Rules To Love By

Quite literally, if you want to experience the joy of lasting marital love with your wife, then you need to act more lovingly toward her. Just Do It! Be affectionate, even if you don't feel like it.

The Importance Of Priorities

This last semester a young woman in one of my classes was lamenting the fact that her boyfriend (who was living a couple hundred miles away) kept telling her that he just didn't have the time to e-mail her very often or to Skype with her very much or to send her little love notes (or even an occasional Hallmark card) letting her know how important she was to him—he was simply "too busy." This was obviously upsetting to her, and as she lamented the fact that the man she loved did not have time for her, a young man in the class suddenly exclaimed: "What if he really is that busy? You know, sometimes we have things to do other than pay attention to you!"

> *I have always thought the actions of men the best interpreters of their thoughts.*
> -John Locke

Needless to say, a "lively discussion" broke out in class that day, and we ended up talking extensively about priorities. The bottom line of that discussion is this: as human beings, we make time for our priorities. Each of us ends up juggling lots of responsibilities in our lives, but we generally do what is necessary to make room for those things that are really important to us. We see to it that we have time for our highest priorities.

> *We all find time to do what we really want to do.*
> -William Feather

And so there are probably some tough questions that we could ask ourselves. For example, where is my wife on my list of priorities? Just how busy am I when it comes to talking with her, spending time with her, letting her know just how important she is to me? The answers to these questions will give each of us a pretty good indication of just how special our wives are in our lives.

Love Doesn't Happen In A Vacuum

As much as we might like to have our relationships exist in a vacuum—to be able to put everything on hold while we simply enjoy the undivided company of the love of our life—it just doesn't work that way. We still have jobs to go to and homes to maintain and cars to keep running and children to raise (and on and on). And in the middle of all these many demands on our lives, the decision to love again, to be affectionate, can so easily be disregarded.

> 🍂
>
> *One of the great illusions of our time is that love is self-sustaining. It is not. Love must be fed and nurtured, constantly renewed. That demands ingenuity and consideration, but first and foremost, it demands time.*
>
> -David Mace

When the toilet backs up, it is hard to think about cuddling with your wife. When there are bills to pay (and more on the way), it is easier to sit mindlessly in front of the television than to go for a gentle walk together around a lake. When there are dishes to do and a lawn to mow and rooms to be painted, it is difficult to take the time for a kiss that is longer than a mere peck.

> 🍂
>
> *Love doesn't grow on trees like apples in Eden — it's something you have to make. And you must use your imagination to make it too, just like anything else.*
>
> -Joyce Cary

When the demands of life are nipping at us from all sides like piranhas, it is tough to focus on surprising her with flowers or leaving a little "I love you" post-it note on the bathroom mirror or placing a "you mean the world to me" card on the pillow. And in the end, even though none of us wants it to happen, when we cease to let the love of our life know that she is just that, the inevitable happens—no matter how deep the love at the outset, that love will slowly become but a faint memory in the marriage.

Rules To Love By

People do not "fall out of love" with each other. When love begins to wane, it is because the marriage has taken a back seat on our list of priorities.

Make your marriage a high priority in your life. Let your wife know—often and in a variety of ways— just how much you love her.

I have seen it so often that it should no longer affect me, but I am still saddened when I see a couple for whom there are no overt destructive behavior patterns in their relationship—no intense anger, no alcoholism, no chronic depression, no debilitating anxiety—and yet their love for one another has begun to shrivel. So often they are good people who really have had a deep love for one another, but they have somehow allowed that love to dim. They have gotten so wrapped up in the many other demands of life that they have lost sight of what encouraged them to say "yes, until death do us part" in the first place.

This has unfortunately become so common that on dozens of occasions my students have expressed confusion and concern when they note the lack of overt affection among couples in their 30s, 40s, and 50s. They are bewildered and sometimes a little frightened. "How can this happen? How can people marry for love only to experience so little of it in their marriage a few years later?" When they do see "an older couple" holding hands or hugging each other or exchanging a kiss, they immediately assume that this couple must not be married (or at least not to each other). And they are increasingly fearful that they, too, may end up on this lonely road.

On occasion students will see my wife and me walking arm in arm in the neighborhood or holding hands at an event on campus, and it is not unusual for them to say something like the following: "Oh, Dr. Buri, that was so cute when we saw you and your wife holding hands at the basketball game the other night." And my response is always the same: "You know, it shouldn't ac-

> *The amount of people in London who flirt with their own spouses is perfectly scandalous. It looks so bad. It is simply washing one's clean linen in public.*
>
> -Oscar Wilde

tually be 'cute' when you see a married couple in their 50s holding hands. In reality, it should be normal!"

Why Marry For Love And Then Not Love?

Whether you are just beginning your marital journey or you have already logged several years together, the research is clear: anyone who wants a successful, loving, life-giving marriage needs to express affection and express it often. These reminders of our love should certainly be a common occurrence at home, but they should also be customary in all sorts of public settings as well—when we are out eating, out shopping, out walking. I am not referring here to sloppy, groping, lascivious PDAs ("public displays of affection"), but I am suggesting that there be gentle, frequent, *and* obvious public declarations that this is the woman I love.

> *Happy marriages begin when we marry the one we love, and they blossom when we love the one we married.*
>
> -Sam Levinson

Some people who have slowly over the years "fallen out of love" by failing to show the person they love that this is in fact the case, have at times despairingly asked me if there is hope for their marriage. Is it worth it? Is their marriage worth fighting for? Let me tell you that I don't believe it is ever too late to save a marriage that has not been riddled by deep-seated character flaws. I have seen apparently lifeless marriages come alive when people have been willing to take a chance—when they have been willing to reach out over the dead space in their relationship and risk being affectionate.

> *You can give without loving, but you cannot love without giving.*
>
> -Amy Carmichael

This may sound strange, but to do this is no small thing. It takes courage to express affection in the face of possible (and sometimes likely) rejection. And to do it over and over again until the sparks of love are re-ignited is nothing short of courageous. As I have said to more than one couple: "Do you have the courage to persist in loving one another? If it has taken you years to suck the life out of your marriage by failing to love because you didn't think of it or because you didn't feel like it or because it wasn't convenient, are you willing to spend same number of years consistently expressing your love one another in order to restore it?"

> *There is comfort in the strength of love; 'twill make a thing endurable which else would overset the brain, or break the heart.*
>
> -William Wordsworth

Some may decide that the deep affection they have had for the love of their life is not worth fighting for. I don't believe this. Lasting marital love has an invigorating and life-giving quality to it. It is frequently the very thing that enlivens our resolve to do battle with those many piranhas nipping at our heels. It is this very affection that will often see us through the most difficult times in our lives. There is strength and beauty in lasting marital love, and it is worth fighting for.

Rules To Love By

Decidedly in this country we marry for love, and therefore it makes perfect sense to express that love for your wife—express it clearly, express it openly, and express it often.

Why would we marry for love and then not?

A Threefold Cord

There is a scripture passage that I have enjoyed for quite a few years now. It is from Ecclesiastes: "Two are better than one...For if they fall, the one will lift up his fellow... And if one prevail against him, two shall withstand him; and a threefold cord is not easily broken" (4: 9-10, 12).

My wife's family is in the twine business, and I spent many long hours as a young man unloading twine from the bowels of barges docked along the Iowa shores of the Mississippi

River. It was then that I first realized how thin and frail each strand of twine actually is. Individually, each fiber of rope will give way rather easily, with relatively little strength to withstand a heavy load. But when the individual fibers are woven together, the resulting tenacity is impressive.

So it is with marriage. Better two than one alone. When one falls, the other is there to help. When there is adversity, the two together will be better able to stand firm. But even better is a threefold cord—even better is a marriage where husband and wife are intertwined with God. This is at the heart of successful marriages—a man, a woman, *and* God. A threefold cord is not easily broken.

Many people find it surprising that the evidence deriving from psychological studies confirms this fact. Each semester in the marriage and family class I teach, students are asked to do a pro / con paper. In other words, based on the psychological research literature, what is the pro-marriage evidence for a particular behavior versus what evidence exists that this behavior undermines marital success? Each semester, someone will want to do this paper on the success of marriages as impacted by participating in religious services and the importance of a personal connection with God. I enthusiastically encourage them to do so.

Inevitably, within a week or two of researching the topic, the student will come back to tell me: "Dr. Buri, I can't find any negatives. All the research evidence points to the positive effects on marriage of both going to church and of having a connection with God. Unless I'm missing something, all the evidence seems to be saying that if you want a successful marriage, then you should be religiously active and you should make God an important part of your love for one another." I always reassure them that they aren't missing anything.

In reality, virtually every study ever done investigating the importance of religion in marital success has confirmed that if you want a long-term, stable, loving, and satisfying marriage, then you should be religiously active and you should make connecting with God a priority in your life.[13] Such consistent findings from empirical research studies often surprise people, but they shouldn't. After all, a primary difference between God and us as human beings is that God loves all the time. It is only reasonable, therefore, that since love is at the heart of every successful marriage, if we want to come closer to loving as God loves—all the time—then getting closer to God will help to make that a reality.

CHAPTER #3

Talk To Me Like You Love Me

One Of The First Things To Go Is Courtesy

Imagine that good friends have invited you to their home for dinner and because of heavy traffic you end up getting to their house half an hour late. As you walk in the front door, the host disgustedly greets you with: "Where have you been? Dinner's been ready for over 25 minutes. What did you think, that we could just sit and wait all night for you to get here?"

Or imagine that after dinner, your host looks out the window and notices that you left your car lights on and with an exasperated sigh, exclaims: "I don't know what is wrong with you. Weren't you thinking when you got here? Now I suppose that when your car won't start because of your carelessness, you'll want me to go out and help you get it started!"

> *I don't know why people should feel that because they have married, they may give up all pretense of good manners and treat their partners as an "old shoe."*
>
> -Emily Post

No doubt such comments would come as quite a surprise. They would probably leave you wondering just what kind of friend is this anyway. And yet, this is exactly the type of exchange that is all too common among married couples.

Good manners, politeness, and common courtesy are some of the first things to disappear from relationships after couples marry.[1] Things we would never say to a guest end up being blurted out unwittingly to a spouse. Isn't it odd that a guest will often be afforded greater kindness than we show the love of our lives? Is it any wonder that the luster of marital bliss begins to dull soon after the wedding vows have been consummated?

> ❦
>
> *The secret of a happy marriage is*
> *simple: just keep on being as polite*
> *to one another as you are to your friends.*
>
> -Robert Quillen

As If He Had Flipped A Switch

I was recently talking with a mortgage broker about the possibility of refinancing our house through his company. As I sat in his office, I was struck by his friendliness and his seemingly genuine interest in me. He was quite engaging as he responded to my refinancing questions, interspersing personal questions of his own about me and about my family.

At one point in our conversation he received a phone call that he apologetically explained he needed to answer. The telephone call was from his wife and the ensuing conversation was anything but warm; in fact, por-

> ❦
>
> *The way we love is not working anymore.*
> *Hardly anyone will challenge that. Hard*
> *evidence convicts it in our lives, our*
> *hearts, our divorce courts. Recalling*
> *author Kurt Vonnegut's wry appeal,*
> *"Please, a little less love, and a little*
> *more common decency," we might won-*
> *der if the way we love is really love at all.*
>
> -Bruce Brander

tions of it could only be described as nasty. Quite honestly, I was relieved when the conversation only lasted a few minutes.

As the man hung up the phone, I wondered which person would turn to face me: the one who had been warm and engaging with me, or the one who had been cold and unpleasant with his wife. As he turned in his chair, it was as if he had flipped a switch and he was again the positive, pleasant, and engaging person that he had previously been with me. The contrast between the way in which he had talked to his wife and the way in which he talked with me was stark. And I found myself wondering how often it is that a mere acquaintance at work receives greater kindness than does the

Marital partnership presents manifold rights and privileges, but bad manners are not among them. Intimacy need not be rude.

-Frank Pittman

love of one's life at home. How often are we more harsh and short and demeaning with the woman we claim to love than we would ever be with a customer at work?

But When Do I Get To Be Myself?

One of the primary culprits in the destruction of marital happiness is the presence of negativity between husbands and wives—the snide comment, the critical glance, the negative tone of voice, the disgusted folding of the arms, the curt request, the rolling of the eyes, the cold glare, the nasty remark.... and the list goes on. So much of married life is everyday, ordinary love. It is lived out in the tiny, mundane, day-in and day-out exchanges between a husband and a wife, and if these exchanges are marked more by negativity and unpleasantness than they are by courtesy and kindness, then an erosion of love in that marriage is inevitable.[2] Negativity will slowly and predictably suck the love (and the life) out of any marriage.

Those people who think good sex is more important to a marriage than good manners will find they are wrong.

-Hubert Downs

And while it is true that the negativity of both wives and husbands will undermine marital happiness, it may surprise you to find out that the negativity of husbands more powerfully undermines marriage than does the negativity of wives.[3] We men may not want to admit it, but we have tremendous power in our marriages. We have the power to breathe life into them through our kindness, courtesy, and warmth. And we have the power to choke off the love on which our marriages will thrive through our cynicism, rudeness, and negativity.

I can already hear the silent protest of some readers: "Do you mean to tell me that after spending my whole day at work being understanding and considerate, I have to go home and be just as pleasant there? When do I get to simply be myself?" To put it bluntly, if any one of us is a jerk, then never! If a man's customary way of relating lacks kindness and is marked by unpleasantness, then he has some serious changing to do. The last thing his marriage needs is for him to be himself.

> 🐚
>
> *Why get married if not to enjoy the pleasure of having another human being treat us as if we are God's gift to humanity?*
>
> -Ellen Sue Stern

The 5:1 Ratio

The research here is extremely clear (and I might add, extremely reasonable). Day after day, we (literally) have hundreds of "moments" with our wives. And what we convey in each of these moments really does matter.

As a brief illustration, let's look at just a few fairly typical moments that a man might have with his wife. When she issues a request, do we act put out, or do we gladly offer our assistance? When she wants to talk about the events of her day, are we disinterested, or do we decide to actually listen to what she has to say? Do we give an eye roll to some comment she makes, or do we hear her out and actually try to understand what she is saying? Do we meet her after a long day with an air of unpleasantness, or do we greet her with a disposition of "I'm glad to see you"? Do we sit with her watching television, bored with the company, or do we do what is needed to enliven even this mundane moment at the end of the day? Are we consistently unresponsive to her desire

> 🐚
>
> *How we talk to each other reflects the quality of our relationship as well as the depth of our character.*
>
> -Dan Allender & Tremper Longman

for conversation, or do we gladly invite the opportunity to connect with the woman we love? Are we repeatedly silent and pre-occupied when we are with her, or do we decide to actually be present to this special person in our lives? Moment by moment, is she greeted by a sour disposition and a facial expression to match, or does she find in us a husband who is pleasant, positive, and upbeat?

Rudeness is the cancer that devours love.

-Dale Carnegie

These moment-by-moment decisions—will I be a pleasant companion to my wife or will I checker our time together with an overriding negativity?—really do have significant and highly predictable consequences in our marriages. In fact, the consequences are so predictable that this one variable—how many positive exchanges couples have in their marriage versus how many negative exchanges they have—prognosticates a happy marriage with amazing accuracy.

I have never known what it was to separate esteem from love.

-Jane Austen

It may surprise you (I know it typically does my students), but we are able to predict a happy marriage (using just this one variable) with much greater accuracy than meteorologists are able to predict the weather. If we want a happy marriage, then day in and day out we need to have at least five positive moments with the woman we love for every negative moment that happens between us. This 5:1 ratio of positive to negative exchanges predicts happy marriages with greater than 90% accuracy.[4]

Rules To Love By

We men do have tremendous power in our marriages—power to be attentive, to listen, to build up, to encourage, to express appreciation. And also the power to be inattentive, to be disinterested, to tear down, to be impatient, to be uncaring. And these moment-by-moment decisions of how we are going to relate to the love of our lives do have predictable consequences.

Granted, we all have those times when we are inclined to exude a certain degree of negativity—after all, we are human. But in the long run, if we want a happy marriage, then these sour times have to decrease in our lives.

If we want an enduring love with that special woman we married—a love that will last a lifetime (and most of us do[5])—then we need to accentuate the positive and eliminate the negative.

Expectations

I am convinced that most of us men are well-intentioned as we enter marriage. It is actually rather unusual to find a man who heads into his marriage with plans to do anything that would intentionally undermine the closeness between him and his wife. Instead, we enter marriage like Aaron (my son's roommate from college mentioned in the first chapter), holding our wives in esteem and valuing them as special in our lives. We really do want our marriages to flourish.

> ॐ
> *Hell is paved with good intentions, not with bad ones. All men mean well.*
>
> -George Bernard Shaw

And yet, many of us get sidetracked. As with most areas of life, good intentions alone are not sufficient to bring about what we desire. Some of us men are plagued by personal demons that threaten to douse the flames of love in our marriages—fits of anger, bouts of discouragement, excessive use of alcohol, addictive behavior. If this is you, prepare yourself to do battle with those demons. And get the help you need.[6]

However, for most of us men, it is not so much the blatant destructive behavior patterns that snuff out that love in our marriages. Instead, it is the little drip (like a leaky faucet) that slowly extinguishes the flame of love that burned so brightly when we said "I do." I have known many young men (more than I would like to count) who began their marriages with high hopes for a growing closeness with their wives, only to find that the price they needed to pay to nourish that closeness was more than they had anticipated. And in the face of such a realization, many of these young men have ended up scaling back on their expectations for marital love.

Remember, our conduct is influenced not by our experience, but by our expectations.

-George Bernard Shaw

Holding One Another To High Expectations

Some might argue that such lowered expectations are a natural and reasonable response to the reality of marriage in 21st century American culture—after all, if you lower you expectations, then you will experience fewer times in your marriage when those expectations aren't met and therefore you will have fewer occasions of marital disappointment. But in actuality, the research has confirmed just the opposite.

Our environment, the world in which we live and work, is a mirror of our attitudes and expectations.

-Earl Nightingale

As it turns out, those couples who lower their expectations for their marriage end up less satisfied with their life together. When they settle for less, allowing negativity and harshness and irritability to become a regular part of their marriage, then marital dissatisfaction is highly predictable. But when couples hold themselves to a higher standard—when they expect that civility and courtesy and kindness will mark their day-to-day interactions and when they are committed to helping one another meet those expectations—then they are far more apt to experience a lasting love in their marriage.[7]

Two authors succinctly summarized this line of research when they wrote: "People with the highest expectations for their marriage usually wind up with the highest-quality marriages.... By holding your relationship to high standards, you are far more likely to achieve the kind of marriage you want than you are by looking the other way and letting things slide.... The couples we studied who adjusted to high levels of negativity...in their marriage ended up less happy or satisfied years later. Those who refused to put up with lots of negativity—who insisted on gently confronting each other when [it] threatened to become pervasive, wound up happy and satisfied years later."[8]

> ౮
>
> *Tolerance is a tremendous virtue, but the immediate neighbors of tolerance are apathy and weakness.*
>
> -James Goldsmith

We Are Not Intentional Marriage Slackers

Recently I was giving a talk to a large group of engaged couples, and I asked the men in the group the following questions: "How many of you are looking forward to being emotionally disconnected from your wives? How many of you are looking forward to that process of gradually growing apart from her rather than growing together? How many of you are looking forward to distancing yourselves from the woman you love? How many of you are looking forward to being married, but disconnected from the person with whom you want to spend the rest of your lives?" Needless to say, hands were not shooting into the air (*and* I was receiving quite a few very strange looks as I asked these questions).

It is the rare man who goes into his marriage anticipating an increasing distance and disconnection from the woman he is marrying. It is the rare man who doesn't desire a growing closeness and connection with the love of his life. (And for many of us, this desire is quite deep.)

The secret to having a good marriage is to understand that marriage must be total, it must be permanent, and it must be equal.

-Frank Pittman

So what is it that would lead well-intentioned men to lower their expectations for marriage? If we really do desire a growing closeness with the love of our lives (and most of us do), then what would deter us from pursuing just that? What is the price tag that many of us find so steep, so unreasonable, that we settle for something with the woman we love that is so much less than what we had desired?

Insensitive? Mean-Spirited?

Dan was a man in his early thirties when I first met him. He was a successful manager in a small but rapidly growing company in Minneapolis. Dan told me that when he and his wife, Amy, married at the age of 26, he was "deeply in love" with her and he was sincere in his desire to keep that love alive. He had no intentions of sabotaging Amy's special-ness in his life. And yet, after just a few years, that love had deteriorated drastically. And now things were at a point where Amy was so hurt and disenchanted with their marriage that she had begun to talk of divorce.

It is an easier thing to be a lover than a husband, for the same reason that it is more difficult to be witty everyday than now and then.

-Honore de Balzac

So what happened between the time of Dan's honest professions of love for Amy on his wedding day and the reality of his marriage a mere seven years later? Was it that Dan was an insensitive and unfeeling man who was incapable of nurturing closeness with the woman he loved? Like most of us men, this was not the case. Was he a mean-spirited person who intentionally kept Amy at a distance in an effort to hurt her? Like most of us, that was one of the furthest things from his mind.

Many readers are no doubt familiar with the fact that men have on occasion been accused of being insensitive and hurtful (and much worse), but in reality, the vast majority of us are not. Unfortunately, however, in my experience it has become more and more necessary to explicitly disabuse people (especially a growing number of women) of such assumptions. So therefore, please let me reiterate: Like most of us men, Dan was not an insensitive, unfeeling, mean-spirited, or hurtful individual. Furthermore, these were not the source of his failing marriage.

Keeping Marriage At Arm's Length

But Dan did bring another characteristic into his marriage with him—a characteristic that over the past 25 years has begun to affect more and more young men in this society. And it was this characteristic that contributed greatly to the failing love between him and Amy. Like a growing number of men in this country, Dan wanted to keep his life as unencumbered as possible. Unintentionally (and even in some ways unknowingly), Dan had hoped that he could be married, but not *so married* that is would significantly disrupt the personal level of freedom and comfort that he had come to enjoy. He had hoped that somehow he would be able to be close to Amy, but not *so close* that it would unduly complicate his life.[9]

As Dan put it one day in a moment of truth: "It really wasn't my intention, but I'm coming to see that what I ended up doing is holding my marriage off at arm's length, sort of stiff arming it. I guess in the back of my mind I thought that if I let my marriage get too close, then it would encroach on my life, asking more and more of me until even-

> *Self-interest is the enemy of all true affection.*
>
> -Tacitus

> *Marriage, like a submarine, is only safe if you get all the way inside it.*
>
> - Frank Pittman

tually there wouldn't be any of *my life* left. I guess I was hoping that somehow I would be able to be close to Amy— after all, I love her—but at the same time keep my marriage at a safe distance."

Opportunities For Connection

What Dan had failed to realize was that if he kept his marriage at a distance, then he would also inevitably keep Amy at a distance. Like most of us men as we walk down the aisle on our wedding day, Dan failed to understand just how much of marriage consists of the repeated, day-in and day-out opportunities for connections with his wife. As a result, even though he loved Amy deeply, the actual daily experience of that love ended up being more of an irritant than a joy.

> *Chains do not hold a marriage together. It is threads, hundreds of tiny threads which sew people together through the years. That is what makes marriage last —more than passion or even sex.*
>
> -Simon Signoret

When Dan walked in at the end of the day, he was *annoyed* by the fact that Amy wanted him to be more interested in being with her than with the newspaper. When looking forward to his free time on the weekend, Dan was *upset* that Amy wanted to spend so much of it doing things together. When they were working side by side on a project around the house, Dan was *irritated* that Amy wanted him to take off his headphones so they could experience that time together. When they had a free evening, Dan was *disgruntled* that Amy wanted to spend it talking rather than simply sitting mindlessly in front of the television. When Amy requested help with something she was working on, Dan was *put out* by these perceived intrusions into his time. When Dan was fixing a snack for himself, he was *exasperated* by any suggestion that maybe he fix something for Amy as well. When Amy was hurt that Dan did not remember the key events of her day and didn't sincerely want to know how each of them went, he was *frustrated* that such connection was expected in his marriage.

This man who used to entice the love of his life to enjoy his company was now irritated by all the time he was expected to spend with her. Is it any wonder that Dan and Amy began to experience that transformation which is more startling than any metamorphosis in nature—the transformation of a relationship that was close, caring, and overflowing with love on the wedding day into one that is distant, disengaged, and brimming with disconnection? What a shock to go from a place of special-ness in the eyes of your spouse to a place of being just one more source of irritation in his life.

> *There is little difference in people, but that little difference makes a big difference. That little difference is attitude. The big difference is whether it is positive or negative.*
>
> -W. Clement Stone

As For Me, We Comes First

Admittedly, it took quite of bit of discussion (between the two of us as well as between him and Amy) before Dan began to see that if he continued to hold off his marriage, then he would also end up holding off the love of his life. It took some time for him to realize that if he was oblivious to (or worse yet, overtly resistant to) the many opportunities for connection with Amy, then he would not simply be maintaining the status quo in their relationship, but he would actually be actively contributing to the widening distance between them. While it had seemed to Dan that his life would be so much less encumbered if he could avoid the entangling connections of married life, he slowly came to acknowledge that if he really did want to have the kind of marriage he had hoped for, then his concern for "me" was going to have to give way to a desire for "we."

> *You can never be happily married to another until you get a divorce from yourself. Successful marriage demands a certain death to self.*
>
> -Jerry McCant

The process of coming to understand himself and his marriage so clearly was obviously a struggle for Dan, but he confided that the biggest part of the struggle was not really a matter of understanding at all—he admitted that he had begun to understand what was needed in his marriage soon after we began to talk months earlier. Like most men, Dan is a bright guy, and so he was able to fairly quickly comprehend the changes that he needed to make in his marriage. Understanding was the easy part.

The Heart Of The Matter

But what Dan really wrestled with, he confessed, was just how much these changes in his marriage were going to require of him. He knew he loved Amy, and he knew that he wanted to continue to hold her in esteem and to value her in his life. But if he actually came out and acknowledged the fact that the way to nurture that special-ness was by treating her as someone who is special—not just once in a while or not just on special occasions, but consistently, moment by moment, day after day, embracing, initiating, and enjoying the many opportunities for connection with her—then he was going to have to make some fairly major changes in his life. Being a man of his word (as most men are), if he actually did admit that he understood what was needed to bring his marriage alive, then it was going to cost him.

> *Marriage is not a noun; it's a verb. It isn't something you get; it's something you do. It's the way you love your partner everyday.*
>
> -Barbara De Angelis

Fortunately, Dan came to the decision that the love of his life was worth it. And being a capable man (which most of us are), Dan has begun the process of giving himself not only to Amy, but to his marriage as well.[10] He is rapidly finding more and more ways to connect with Amy, letting her know over and over again (and typically without ever explicitly saying it) just how special she is in his eyes. And as is true of virtually all marriages in which men respond as Dan is respond-

> *There is no more lovely, friendly, and charming relationship, communion, or company than a good marriage.*
>
> -Martin Luther

ing, his marriage is flourishing—it is becoming what he had always hoped it would be.[11]

To love means to decide independently
to live with an equal partner, and to
subordinate oneself to the formation
of a new subject, a "we."

-Fritz Kunkel

SENSIBLE EFFORT
BY REASONABLE PEOPLE

- **Be someone who is enjoyable to be with**
  - o **Be courteous**
  - o **Do not be rude**
  - o **Be patient**
  - o **Do not be easily irritated**
  - o **Be upbeat**
  - o **Do not be moody**
  - o **Be kind**
  - o **Do not be nasty**

- **Take advantage of the many opportunities for connection with the love of your life everyday**
  - o **Spend free time with her**
  - o **Redecorate together**
  - o **Help her with her projects**
  - o **Shop together**
  - o **Ask if you can get her something**
  - o **Plan for the weekend together**
  - o **Do weekly household chores together**
  - o **Clean up after dinner together**
  - o **Take a sincere interest in her day**

Kindness is the life's blood, the elixir
of marriage. Kindness makes the
difference between passion and caring.

-Randolph Ray

Not The Stuff Of Rocket Science

I doubt that this will come as a surprise to anyone, but the very behaviors that led us down the path of loving someone in the first place are the same behaviors that are needed if that love is to grow.[12] It is not as if the initial stages of love require one set of interactions—courtesy , kindness, consideration, mutual interest, connection—but then once the love is established, a new set of behaviors are necessary—rudeness, impatience, distance, selfishness, disconnection.

Much of what we need to do to promote love in our marriage is not all that complicated—it is not the stuff of rocket science. We are not delving into some deep mysteries of love that require special intelligence to understand or unique powers to implement.

> ॐ
> *If couples would put half the effort into marriage that they put into courtship, they would be surprised how things will brighten up.*
>
> -Billy Graham

Would you ever fall in love with someone who is inconsiderate toward you, who doesn't want to be bothered by your requests for assistance, who seldom gives any indication of joy to see you, who is more interested in the television than in you? I certainly hope not! Most of us understand what is necessary for love to develop, and we are capable of making that love happen. After all, we fell in love, didn't we? So for most of us, what threatens to erode the love in our marriages is more a matter of self-interest than ineptitude, more a matter of unwillingness than ignorance, and more a matter of indolence than inadequacy.

The Currents Of Life

Have you ever noticed how busy life can be? Like the currents of a fast-moving river, life just continues its flow, often tugging us along with it. The demands of life never stop. And if we allow the resulting busy-ness to pull us and our marriages along unchecked, then we can expect some unpleasant consequences. And sometimes these consequences can be devastating.

❦

Marriage must constantly fight against a monster which devours everything: routine.

-Honore de Balzac

Take for example Al and Sarah. This couple met through a mutual friend a few years after graduating from college. They hit it off right away and as they began to spend more and more time together, they discovered that they had a lot in common. They both enjoyed outdoor sports, they both kept abreast of current events, both of them were avid readers, they both liked going to professional sporting events (especially the Minnesota Twins), and both of them loved going out for quiet dinners with a good bottle of wine. It seemed that they were never at a loss for things they enjoyed doing together or topics they enjoyed discussing, and as they allowed their lives to become more and more entwined, it was only a matter of time before both of them found it difficult to think about living life without the other. Al and Sarah had fallen in love. So, naturally, they decided to get married.

> ☙
> *The tragedy of Western marriages is that most of us quit courting once we're married.*
> -James Smith

During their early years of marriage, Al and Sarah easily built on the many areas of connection they had already experienced. They continued to find lots of time for each other, enjoying long discussions, quiet dinners, jogging, backpacking, and Twins games. Their life together as a married couple just seemed to be a natural extension of the love they had cultivated before marriage.

Unfortunately, however, like many couples who have been married for a number of years, Al and Sarah slowly began to carve out less and less time in their lives for each other. At first it was work—as they each experienced success in their respective careers, they began to spend more and more time in the workplace until, like many Americans, they began to give the best of themselves each week to their jobs.[13] And then the children came along, first Jack and then Allie.[14] Coming home each night to children who needed what felt like the last of their time and energy, Al and Sarah ended up saving less and less for each other.

> ☙
> *If your job gets your best energy, your marriage will wither.*
> -Linda & Charlie Bloom

All He Wanted Was To Sit And Mush

As is so often the case, the changes Al and Sarah experienced in their marriage were so gradual that they were hardly noticeable. Al failed to realize that he and Sarah had begun to spend less and less time together, that they had begun to quietly watch television during times when they used to have lively discussions about a variety of topics, that he had gradually become "too tired" to go backpacking with Sarah or to read a book and discuss it with her or to simply go out for a peaceful dinner for two. It was just so much easier for Al to come home, get into something comfortable, and just unwind. Life was so busy for him and

There is a time when we must firmly choose the course we will follow, or the relentless drift of events will make the decision for us.

-Herbert V. Prochnow

seemed to be asking so much of him that once he got home, all he wanted to do was "sit and mush" and do as little as possible. Needless to say, the currents of life were beginning to sweep away the love that Al and Sarah experienced in their marriage.

I work just a couple of blocks from the Mississippi River and for years I have gotten my exercise by jogging on the road that runs along the bluff above the river. On many days when I have been jogging during the late spring or early fall, crew teams from local universities have been practicing on the river. Occasionally one of these teams will take a brief break and stop rowing. Over and over again, the result is always the same. As soon as they have stopped rowing, they lose their momentum as the currents of the river begin to pull them downstream.

Rules To Love By

Your marriage and my marriage are just like this. The currents of life are working against us. Each of us in our own way is rowing upstream. Each of us is fighting against the currents of life that seek to slowly pull our marriages downstream.[15]

If we cease to row, if we choose to repeatedly sit and mush and do as little as possible in our marriages, then the currents of life will win...and you and I (and our marriages) will lose.

We Used To Have So Much In Common

Al had slowly allowed himself to slip into a relatively passive position in his marriage. His life was so busy and the level of responsibility he needed to carry was so taxing that it seemed only reasonable to assume a place at home that would require him to give less and less of himself to his marriage.

Love endures only when the lovers love many things together and not merely each other.

-Walter Lippmann

But the strange thing (at least from Al's perspective) was that even though he had come to a place of investing less of his time and energy at home, it was not a situation with which he was happy. As Al put it one day: "In a lot of ways, I just don't get it. Sarah and I used to have so much in common. We loved to do everything together—walk in the woods, go to a ballgame, read a book, watch a movie, go jogging, enjoy a long quiet dinner for two. But now, it seems that all we do together is get the kids to their next event and all we seem to talk about is who's responsible for what. It's weird—and it sucks! This is not at all what I was looking for. We're married and we have a house and we have children together, but it feels like we have less in common now than we did when we were dating."

Early Warning Signs

My wife and I have had many years of teenage drivers in our family, and there have been stretches of time where I would end up not driving one of our cars for days (and sometimes even weeks). During these times I would encourage our children to listen for any unusual sounds coming from the engine and to pay attention to any dashboard gauges that might light up as they were driving. It was my hope that if a problem with the car did arise, we could head it off before it became a more serious problem.

Every marriage ought to be equipped with a built-in early warning system that lets you know when your marital quality is in danger of deteriorating. I call this system the Marital Poop Detector because it's really a way of saying something just doesn't smell right.

-John M. Gottman

Unfortunately on more than one occasion, once I did have the opportunity to drive the car again, I was surprised to hear grinding brakes (all the way to the rotors), to notice a strong pull of the steering wheel (from a front end that had hit one too many Minnesota potholes), or to see the hot light start blinking shortly after turning the ignition key (from a leak in a radiator hose). Typically I was quite perplexed that no one had noticed any of the early warning signs of an emerging problem.

Our marriages are often the same—there are early warning signs indicating that actions are necessary if more serious problems are to be averted.[16] How often I have wished that we men were as sensitive to the warning signs in our marriages as we are to the warning signs in our cars. And specifically with Al, how I wished he had been more attentive to the early warning signs in his marriage. Maybe then he could have headed off the more serious problems that now threatened to destroy his life together with Sarah.

Some Devastating Consequences

It had started innocently enough. An occasional conversation with an attractive co-worker named Nikki, at first when passing one another in the hallway, then during a break over coffee. Gradually these apparently innocuous conversations at work became more and more frequent…and more and more enjoyable.

> *I'm tempted to go to all the buildings downtown and put up a sign. "DAN-GER ZONE: Men and Women at Work." Today's workplace is the most common breeding ground for affairs. It's the proximity and collegiality --- the intimacy of working together, not bad marriages, that is the slippery slope to infidelity.*
>
> -Shirley Glass

While Al's conversations with Sarah at home seemed to be stuck on things like when he would be home, what needed to be fixed, and who in the family needed to be where when, his conversations with Nikki seemed to flow easily from one topic to the next. They talked about other people in the office, the general work conditions in the company, problems with management—they had a lot in common. And slowly their conversations drifted to more personal topics—their favorite activities, the movies they had seen recently, the books they were reading, their career aspirations, *and* their disappointments at home.

Your Thought Life (It Does Have A Life): What Are You Feeding It?

Al had never set out to have Nikki take the place of companionship in his life that had so clearly been Sarah's. He had never intended that he would anticipate his times with Nikki more than he would look forward to spending time with his wife. He was even at first surprised to find himself comparing Sarah with Nikki. But rather than fighting off such thoughts (where the deck was so clearly stacked against Sarah), Al began to entertain them more and more frequently. Rather than starving these thoughts, nipping them in the bud, Al fed them. More and more he allowed himself to wonder: What would it be like to be with Nikki anytime he wanted?

What would it be like to come home to Nikki rather than Sarah? What would it be like to make love to Nikki rather than his wife? And the inevitable happened.[17]

It had never been Al's plan to cheat on his wife, but he had ignored so many obvious warning signs in his marriage that his infidelity should not have come as a surprise to anyone. Al had failed to notice the growing distance between him and the woman who was the love of his life. As with my children who seemed so oblivious to the grinding brakes, I found myself incredulously asking Al: "How could you not notice? How could you not be aware of what was happening in your marriage? How could you be so busy, so preoccupied, so oblivious, so negligent that you couldn't see that the love of your life was slipping away?"

SENSIBLE EFFORT
BY REASONABLE PEOPLE

- What is it that you and your wife have enjoyed doing together? Is it:
  - o Dancing?
  - o Biking?
  - o Going to a concert?
  - o Playing tennis?
  - o Jogging?
  - o A quiet dinner?
  - o Walks in the park?
  - o Camping?
  - o The club scene?
  - o Going to church?
  - o Sailing?
  - o Going to a ball game?
  - o Skiing?
  - o Going on a picnic?
  - o Canoeing?
  - o Getting together with friends?
  - o Playing softball?
  - o Reading a book together?
  - o Going to a movie?

Whatever these activities have been, continue to enjoy them with the love of your life. And be open to new ones that you can enjoy together.

Don't Try, Do!

The roads we take are more important than the goals we announce. Decisions determine destiny.

-Frederick Speakman

It is often difficult to make the time in our lives to simply enjoy activities together. Trust me, I know how tough this can be. I am well aware of all the forces working against us here—lack of time, lack of money, lack of energy. But if we don't work to preserve these times together, if we don't continue to enjoy these activities with the love of our life, then the very things that led us to marry her in the first place will be swept away with the currents of life.

❦

Decision is a sharp knife that cuts clean and straight; indecision, a dull one that hacks and tears and leaves ragged edges behind it.

-Gordon Graham

On more than one occasion, when I have encouraged a man to invest greater time and energy in making these activities with his wife happen, my words of advice have been met with a lackluster response. Seldom has this response taken the form of explicit resistance. In fact, seldom have I met overt resistance from a man in virtually any area where he has received suggestions for change that will improve his marriage. More often, the response is one that affords wiggle room, one that suggests: "I'll see what I can do—I'll try."

Now it has been my experience that most of us are men of integrity—we are true to our word. If we say we will do something, then most often, we will. So when a man tells me, "I'll do it," then I'm pretty sure that he will. But if he tells me, "I'll try," then I am doubtful that much of anything is really going to happen. I am reminded of Yoda's response to Luke Skywalker in *Star Wars* when Luke commented that he would try. Yoda stated: "Do or do not, there is no try!"

❦

Knowing is not enough, we must apply. Willing is not enough, we must do.

-Johann von Goethe

Rules To Love By

No matter how busy we are or how burdened we become with the responsibilities of life, if we are to realize the successful, happy, and loving marriage we envisioned when we said "I do," then we cannot allow the currents of life to sweep away those activities that have brought us so much enjoyment with the woman we love.

Make a decision (make it often if you have to) that you will continue to initiate those mutually enjoyable times that made this woman special in your life. Don't simply try—do !

CHAPTER #4

Keeping The Flames Of Love Alive

You Look Wonderful Tonight

A close friend of mine (Todd) had dated many women as a young man and when he was 24 he began to date the love of his life. He and that special woman (Kristi) have now been married for almost 15 years. One night Todd and I were talking over a couple beers, and I commented to him how impressed I was that he and Kristi had remained so close over all these years. I told him that I was especially impressed by the fact that he still admired Kristi physically. Whether I saw the two of them together or whether Todd was simply talking about Kristi when she wasn't there, it was obvious that she was still "very hot" in his eyes.

I was rather surprised by Todd's response. The first thing he said was (and this part was not all that surprising): "I think we better grab a couple more beers before we start talking about this one." And so we did, and then Todd proceeded to tell me the story behind the fact that he really did find his wife very attractive.

I am learning about people the hard way, by being one.

-Ashleigh Brilliant

"About 8 years ago I was on a family vacation with Kristi and our children and a song came on the radio. The words of the song went something like this: 'Yes, my darling, you look wonderful tonight!' And as I looked over at Kristi, I realized that I would have a difficult time singing those words to her." At this point, Todd stopped to gather himself. It was clear that this was not an easy thing for him to talk about. Todd proceeded to tell me how after that day in the car, he began to think seriously about why he no longer found Kristi as beautiful as he once had. Did she change all that much? And he had to admit to himself that no, she was still a very attractive woman. And then he confided: "You know, I began to take a cold hard look at myself. Was there something about me that had changed? And over the next several months I slowly began to realize that something had changed."

I will never forget what Todd told me next. He said: "John, what I am about to tell you I have never shared with anyone before, but here goes. When I was a young man, I had dabbled in some pornography, but I stopped when I started dating Kristi—she didn't like it, and besides, I didn't need it. But after we had been married a few years, I ended up going back to the pornography. It started one night when I was up late working on the computer and I stumbled across a website. Well, to make a long story short, I started to use pornography more and more often. I figured that it wouldn't hurt anything as long as Kristi didn't find out. Well, that was when it started—that was when this woman who had been so beautiful to me slowly became less and less attractive in my mind. That was when I slowly became less and less satisfied with this woman who had meant everything to me."

> ෆ
> *Cheap sex and precious love; you can't have one if you have the other.*
> -Jim Conway

She Is One Sexy Woman

Todd and I talked for a long time that night. And as we talked, I mentioned to Todd that what he found out the hard way (personally) has been verified in numerous research studies—when we expose ourselves to physically attractive pornographic women, we begin to find our partners less beautiful and we slowly become less satisfied with them.

> ෆ
> *Experience is a hard teacher because she gives the test first, the lesson afterwards.*
> -Vernon Law

The fact that this had happened to Todd's affection for Kristi was nothing unique or surprising. It is going to happen to those men who use pornography.

But what was unique and surprising about Todd was the fact that he was so reflective and that he had the capacity to be brutally honest with himself. Most men who use pornography are not typically aware of the fact that they are gradually finding their partners less and less attractive. And those who are aware of this happening are quick to deny that pornography has had anything to do with the changes. But Todd was a reflective man. He was willing to spend time with himself thinking about his life, thinking about his decisions, and thinking about his behaviors. He was willing to ask himself some tough questions. He was willing to admit to himself when something about him needed to change.

> ॐ
>
> *Not choice, but habit,*
> *rules the unreflective herd.*
>
> -William Wordsworth

Todd told me that he struggled for some time with the reality of what pornography was doing to his marriage. As he put it: "I knew it was true. I knew what it was doing to my love for Kristi (and I didn't need any research studies to show me). I knew that my use of pornography was slowly sucking the life out of our marriage and I knew that I needed to give it up. But whenever I tried, I found that it had more of a hold on me than I thought. But I knew what I needed to do and I was determined to do it, and I eventually did. I haven't used pornography now for over five years. And, you know, it took a while, but that affection for Kristi slowly came back and now it is better than ever. She is one sexy woman, and she's the only one I need, and she's the only one I want."

> ॐ
>
> *It is not only the most difficult*
> *thing to know oneself, but the*
> *most inconvenient too.*
>
> - Josh Billings

She Is Special And I Want To Keep Her That Way

In my conversation with Todd, I had alluded to research findings suggesting that the use of pornography would not be a good idea for any man who really does see his partner as special and who wants to keep her that way. This particular avenue of research began back in the late 1970s, and it initially consisted of studies in which men were shown pictures and movies of beautiful women and were then asked to judge the attractiveness of other women. What the researchers found was that after viewing these beautiful women, the men's judgments of the attractiveness of other women were more negative. This was termed "the contrast effect"—in contrast to beautiful women, other women will pale by comparison and will end up being evaluated more negatively.[1]

> ℧
>
> *I do not think much of a man who is not wiser today than he was yesterday.*
>
> -Abraham Lincoln

Subsequent investigations of this contrast effect have used pictures of physically attractive women as well as popular erotica. Researchers have found that after repeated exposure to such materials: (a) men judged their current partners as less satisfying, (b) they rated themselves as less in love with their wives, (c) they rated their partners as having less sexual appeal, (d) they reported lower commitment to their partners, and (e) they judged their partners as less attractive and less desirable.[2]

These research findings, along with many more that have since been published[3], should not come as much of a surprise to any of us. Some of us may not want to admit it, but they make perfect sense. As one author stated: "The pornographic woman has advantages. Always available for a sexual encounter, she…is not shy about exposing her body to the man's gaze…. She makes no demands for a committed relationship, she is never sick nor uninterested in sex…and she is always very interested in pleasing a man."[4]

With the incredible availability of pornographic images today, is it any wonder that so many men are turning to pornography? Several marriage and family counselors that I know have commented that more than ever before they find themselves working with marriages that have been riddled by the use of pornography. For lots of us men, it's just easier; it's less of a hassle to engage in sex with this beautiful pornographic image than it is to have sex with our partner. The woman on the screen is so much more available and so much less demanding than is the real woman in our lives who actually wants us to put in the time and the energy to have a relationship to go along with the sex.

> ౘ
> *The sexual act without intimacy retains a separateness that cannot be forgotten by orgasm.*
> -Erich Fromm

Rules To Love By

The number one sexual problem for married couples in this country is a lack of sexual desire for one's spouse.[5]

Protect the beauty of your wife. Do what is necessary to preserve her physical allure. Keep her sexy. Save yourself for her.

About 15 years ago I was giving a talk here in the Twin Cities and during the talk a woman in the audience asked a very personal question. She said: "My husband uses pornography on a regular basis and over the past couple of years he has become more and more critical of my appearance and my ability to perform sexually. Is it possible that his reactions to me are related to his use of pornography?"

As this woman spoke, two things occurred to me. First, it was obvious that there was nothing wrong with her appearance—by any objective standard, she was an attractive woman. Secondly, I was struck by the fact that she must have been quite desperate; after all, she had asked such a personal question in an auditorium full of people. And as I walked away that night, I found myself wondering how many women are out there living with the degrading effects of pornography that is being used by the men who claim to love them.

Would You Go To Bed With Me?

One of my favorite psychological studies of all time was carried out on a college campus. In this study, an attractive, well-dressed young man walked up to college co-eds and said: "Hello, I think you are very attractive. Would you go to bed with me?" None of the young women who were approached agreed to these sexual advances. The researchers then reversed this scenario: an attractive, well-dressed young woman walked up to male students on campus and said: "Hello, I think you are very attractive. Would you go to bed with me?" Fully 75% of these male students said yes.[6]

Sometimes when I have talked about this study in class, both the women and the men express some surprise at these findings, but usually for different reasons. Typical of women's surprise is the response of one young woman who exclaimed: "Do you mean to tell me that 75% of men are willing to have sex with someone they have just met, simply because she is cute and available?" In this particular class there just happened to be a young man who was particularly quick-witted and he immediately responded: "Not necessarily; sometimes she doesn't have to be cute!"

🐚

Love in young men, for the most part, is not love, but simply sexual desire and its accomplishment is its end.

-Cervantes

Men in the classes where we discuss this study will also sometimes express some surprise at these findings, but for a different reason. They are more apt to express surprise that no woman would take advantage of such an opportunity.

Obviously, some rather distinct differences between men and women exist when it comes to sex. A failure to understand

and respond to these differences has tripped up many a man who has declared "I do" to that special woman in his life.

There Is So Much More To Sex Than Just Sex

It is nearly universal in this country that men would like to have sex more often than their partners. In fact, in a large review of the research findings in this area, the following summary statement was offered: "All the evidence we have reviewed points toward the conclusion that men desire sex more than women.... Men want sex more than women at the start of a relationship, in the middle of it, and after many years of it.... We did not find a single study, on any of the nearly dozen different measures, that found women had a stronger sex drive than men. We think that the combined quantity, quality, and convergence of the evidence render the conclusion indisputable."[7]

Arguably one of the best characterizations of this sexual difference between men and women can be found in the movie *Annie Hall*. When a husband and wife are asked (separately) by a therapist how often they have sex, the husband (played by Woody Allen) responds: "Hardly ever, maybe three times a week," and his wife (portrayed by Diane Keaton) responds to the same question by saying: "Constantly, three times a week."

In addition to the desire on the part of men to have sex more often, another rather stark gender difference in sexuality can be

A healthy sexual relationship is one in which the two partners are engaged in the ongoing process of attracting and luring one another to bed.

-Andrew Greeley

found in the fact that the context for sexual desire is often quite different for women than it is for men. For many of us men, there are times when our desire for sex with the woman we love does not go a whole lot deeper than the fact that we would like to have sex. For our wives, however, there is a context for sexual activity that is frequently crucial if their experience of sex is to be an enjoyable one. Several reviews of the literature have emphasized the fact that compared with men, the sexual desire and sexual satisfaction of women is much more linked to the committed, intimate, and romantic nature of the relationship.[8]

Understanding And Responding

Failure to understand these rather dramatic gender differences in sexuality has plagued many marriages in this country. I have on more than one occasion had to encourage wives to appreciate and respond to the sexual desires of their husbands. This encouragement for wives to serve the sexual needs of their husbands has not been without valid concern for the ongoing life of their marriage. A sex researcher recently summarized the relative importance of sex in this way: "Men are more likely than women to use the quality of their sexual relationship as a barometer for the quality of the entire relationship."[9] So despite my justified timidity (such suggestions are often a dangerous thing for a man to propose), it is very important that a woman not minimize the differences between her need for sex in the marriage and that of her husband.[10]

But quite honestly, most of my encouragement to appreciate and respond to the sexual differences between men and women has been directed at us men. This may sound a little blunt—sometimes it's difficult to subtly express something that is so blatantly obvious—but most of us men most of the time overlook the sexual needs of our wives.

It Begins Between The Ears, Not Between The Legs

Take a few moments and remember how you romanced your wife. Do you remember the dinners, the first passionate kiss, the unique getaways together, the first time you touched her body, the long conversations over a bottle of wine, the moonlight walks? (As I write this I must admit that I can vividly recall the first full moon I shared with my wife, even though it was over forty years ago. When I mentioned this to her, she expressed surprise that I was able to remember the moon with all the other things that happened that night.)

We have to realize that we did a lot to win over the love of our lives. And then we need to realize how easy it is to blow it when we exude as much romance as a piece of rice cake. It is not a big turn on for our wives when after a long day of going our separate ways we look over from the television only long enough to say: "Hey, do you want to go do it?" And worse yet is when we have shown the neighbor's dog more attention than we have her, and then we jump into bed with our passions blazing and we can't understand why she isn't as turned on as we are.

If any of us wants to have great sex with our wife, then we are going to have to romance her, and that romancing begins in your own mind. Let me ask you: Do you think up ways to surprise her and to let her know she's special? Do you think about flirting with her the next time you see her? Do you use your imagination to conjure up a unique night out? Do you ever greet her with a kiss that lasts longer than a nanosecond? Do you undress her (rather than some stranger) in your mind's eye? Do you spend time thinking about all the ways in which she is the love of your life?

It is always fascinating to watch a man get involved in an affair—how romantic he becomes, how much time he spends thinking about this new woman, how much energy he invests in her. And I find myself wanting to recommend that we men begin having affairs and that we have them regularly—but that we always have them with the same woman, our wives, the real and time-tested love of our lives.

> *Sex is a conversation carried out by other means. If you get on well out of bed, half the problems of bed are solved.*
>
> -Peter Ustinov

> *The way a man's mind runs is the way he is sure to go.*
>
> -Henry B. Wilson

Have You Ceased Being Lovers?

A former student (from my marriage and family class) stopped by my office one day and in the course of the conversation we talked about his marriage, and he told me that at least two times a year he and his wife have secret rendezvous. He described how they meet each other at a coffee shop or a wine bar after work and how he uses his charm to win her over—basically he "picks her up." They go out on the town together and then they end up going back to "his place" (which is actually their home) or else they end up at some fancy hotel for the night.

It doesn't take much: a shared shower in the morning, a sexy message on the answering machine at work, a little note in the lunchbox, a long hug before we turn off the lights. These are the little things that go a long way.

-Ellen Sue Stern

They have been married for over 10 years and they now have two children, so he admitted that it is becoming a little more difficult to make these clandestine evenings happen, but he was quick to add that he will do whatever it takes to continue to win over the love of his life with nights like these. As he put it, "I was hot after her when we were dating and after all these years, I'm still hot after her and I don't plan to let it die." Needless to say, it was delightful to hear this man talk about his love for the special woman in his life and his desire to keep that love alive.

A Wedding Toast:
Here's to the husband
And here's to the wife;
May they remain
Lovers for life.

-Paul Dickson

Maybe "pick up dates" are a little more than you can handle. Maybe something a little tamer (or less expensive) is your style. For example, I know a couple that twice a month gets their children to bed and then has a romantic candle light dinner in their home. They seldom have the same cuisine twice in a row, and he usually does all the cooking. He told me that he loves to romance his wife (just like he did when they were young lovers) as they share a bottle of wine and spend the evening talking about anything except the current problems encroaching upon their lives.

Regardless of your style or your budget, find ways to fan the flames in your relationship. And let me tell you that sitting around all weekend forty-five pounds overweight in your favorite boxers with a bowl of chips watching one ball game after another will not do the trick.

Love, be true to her, be dear to her;
Health, stay close to her;
Joy, draw near to her,
Search your treasure-house through and through for her,
Follow her footsteps the wide world over.
And keep her husband always her lover!

-Anna Lewis

SENSIBLE EFFORT

BY REASONABLE PEOPLE

If you want a vibrant sex life in your marriage, then it is important to realize that there is a lot more to love-making than mere genital activity. If you want good sex with your wife over many years of marriage, then:

- **Don't assume that it will simply happen**
    - o **It won't—good long-term sex does not simply happen naturally**

- **Give your sexual relationship with your wife the attention it deserves**
    - o **Make it a high priority—"working at" good sex in your marriage is not a contradiction in terms**

- **Be romantic**
  - Find lots of ways (some old, some new) to romance your wife
  - Let her know that you find her attractive
  - Be mindful of what says to her, "You are the love of my life"
  - Make it clear that she is still hot in your eyes—keep the passion alive
  - Romancing her everyday is not too frequent
  - Plan romantic dates—make "the world stop" so that the two of you can simply be together

Romance was never my strong suit. I proposed to my wife Lynne in her parents' garage; I took my Harley-Davidson on our honeymoon; I thought our best anniversary was the one we spent watching a video of Rocky III. But several years into our marriage, I realized that being a [good] husband meant more than bringing home a paycheck and occasionally talking shop with Lynne. I needed to grow in the gentle art of romance.

-Bill & Lynne Hybels

Remember that being lovers is what distinguished this relationship from the many other friendships you've had. Unfortunately, too many of us forget this as we begin to take our wives for granted, and we cease being lovers. And once we do, then we stop holding hands in public, we no longer sit beside each other in the same booth at restaurants, we cease kissing at stop lights and making out in elevators, and (the most disheartening of all) we end up looking more longingly at a passerby than at our partner. Is it any wonder that once a couple has ceased being lovers, they begin to describe their sex life as "boring, dull, monotonous, routine?"[11]

ॐ

People being what they are, it is
no great achievement to woo someone
into a short-lived intimacy. It takes
a great deal more character and
finesse to make a long-term marriage
into a romantic, glowing love affair.

-M. P. Horban

Atrophy Is Not Confined To Body Parts

When I was 33, I ruptured my Achilles tendon while playing basketball. Let me encourage you to avoid this injury if at all possible—it is painful! I went through reconstructive surgery and spent three months in a cast, and when the cast was removed, I was surprised at the atrophy that had occurred in my right leg in such a short period of time. What I found out the hard way is that if you don't use it, you lose it.

Well, what I have come to realize over the years is that atrophy is not confined to body parts. It also applies to marriages. Too many couples find out the hard way that if you don't use it, you lose it. Even though I should be accustomed to it by now (because I see it so often, even with young couples), I am still repeatedly surprised by how many of us settle into a routine of mutual co-existence with the love of our life— "same old, same old"—and then we wonder what happened to the sparks of love in our marriage.

Remember what it took to get this person to fall in love with you in the first place. If you want to keep that love alive, then you are going to have to continue to work at instilling romance into your life together. There are no formulas for success here—this is not a science. What works for you may be insignificant for other couples. Use your imagination and be creative—good sex is rooted in romance, thoughtfulness, and genuine interest in your partner more than it is rooted in sexual technique.[12]

It is always delightful to watch young men and women in love, and because of my job I have the opportunity to see it often. But it is even more delightful to see older men and women in married love, couples who have weathered some of the storms of life and have been able to fall in love with the same person over and over again. For such couples in love (regardless of their age), there is a freshness to their lives. They radiate a hope and an enthusiasm, even in the middle of their struggles. Their love for one another has a life-giving quality to it, certainly invigorating their lives, but also spilling out and bringing life to those around them.

> ꕥ
> *A successful marriage requires falling in love many times, always with the same person.*
>
> -Mignon McLaughlin

Rules To Love By

Most of us know how to be romantic—after all, we've done it many times before—and now it is largely a matter of deciding to be romantic again.

Regardless of whether you are just starting out in your life together or whether you have been married for many years, find ways to repeatedly instill romantic love into your life together. Fall in love with her over and over again.

Do you remember how much time, effort, and energy it took to convince her that you were worth loving? Show her that she was right, not just then, but now, and not just once, but many times.

CHAPTER #5

The Crucible Of Conflict

Most Of Us Are Not Fools

Time and again we have heard that a good marriage doesn't simply happen naturally once the ceremony is finished. We have been told over and over that a good marriage takes work—and lots of it!

And in response, many of us embark upon this marital journey with an understanding that it is going to require quite a bit from us.[1] After all, the reality of the situation is this: we met someone who was a virtual stranger, we fell in love with her, and then we began to graft together two distinct lives so that a satisfying and enduring love could develop. Only a fool would fail to realize the daunting nature of such a task—and quite honestly, most of us are not fools.

And so many of us enter marriage fully aware that this is going to be hard work... It is only later that we discover we have (at best) only a vague notion of the type of work that will be required of us. We find that it is one thing to know that lots of effort is necessary, and it's quite another thing to understand just where in the marriage that effort needs to be expended.

> ☙
>
> *When love and skill work together, expect a masterpiece.*
>
> -John Ruski

One huge problem for many of us is that the marriage license doesn't come with an instruction manual. In fact, it doesn't even come with a quick reference guide for basic information and a few trouble-shooting tips. How much easier this whole marriage thing would be if there were some sort of step-by-step instructions on "how to build it," but that is not reality. Putting together a successful marriage is not like putting together a swing set.

Instead, a successful marriage depends upon the development of particular skill sets. The research is extremely clear. Any couple who wants a happy and long-lasting marriage has to hone certain skills. And it is exactly here—in the development of these skills essential to marital success—that the hard work of marriage hits many of us the hardest. And it is to these skills that we now turn our attention.

Conflict: Is This The Way It's Supposed To Be?

Conflict is an inevitable part of any significant long-term relationship.[2] This is one fact that needs to be firmly established in the consciousness of each of us—conflict in marriage is inevitable.

> ꙮ
> *It is sometimes essential for a husband and a wife to quarrel—they get to know each other better.*
>
> -Johann von Goethe

When this topic comes up in my marriage and family class, most of the students are able to agree with the veracity of this statement. They are able to admit that conflict in marriage does take place. However, many of them are less willing to concede that this is the way it should be. It's as if they have resigned themselves to the fact that married couples will have disagreements, but they are convinced that this is not how married love ought to be.

The same is true for many married couples. We have come to a place of reluctantly conceding that conflict is going to happen in our marriage, but deep down we don't believe that this is the way it's supposed to be.

And herein lies a problem for any couple who truly wants a successful marriage. Basically, if conflict is not valued as a healthy component of marriage and it erupts (which it will in virtually every marriage), then what is an individual left to think? One possibility sounds something like this: "Obviously the love we have is not all that special after all—because people who really love each other don't argue like we do." Or another seemingly logical (albeit faulty) conclusion that often emerges if conflict is not seen as a valuable part of married life takes this form: "I clearly married the wrong person—because if she were the right person, then we wouldn't be disagreeing like this." A third line of reasoning that makes sense if conflict is not seen as a normal, necessary, and healthy part of marriage emerges along these lines: "This arguing is not what I bargained for—if this is what marriage is going to be, then I am not sure this marriage stuff is for me."

It is not difficult to see how such reasoning will have destructive consequences for marital love. If a man doubts the love in his marriage ("the love we have must not be that special after all") or if he doubts his wife ("if she were the right person") or if he doubts his commitment to his marriage ("if this is what marriage means, then I'm not so sure about being married"), then the very foundations on which a lifelong, loving marriage is built will be shaken.[3]

What counts in making a happy marriage is not so much how compatible you are, but how you deal with the incompatibility.

-George Levinger

Rules To Love By

It is the rare man who does not end up coming face to face with the reality of conflict in his marriage. And for most of us, wrestling with that reality is no small thing. Nearly all of us will readily admit that conflict with the love of our lives was not what we thought we signed on for when we said "I do."

But the reality of married love is this: Conflict is inevitable. And not only is it inevitable, but it is also normal, necessary, and healthy. Without this realization—that conflict in marriage is a good thing—then a person will end up doing little more than tolerating that conflict.

Most Of Us Men Avoid

It has been reported that in close to fifteen percent of marriages in this country, the husband and the wife have become acclimated to a fairly high level of disagreement between them. Basically, they have come to see a certain amount of ongoing conflict in their marriage as normal, and therefore, a persistent pattern of quarreling has come to define their relationship. Such marriages have been described as Conflict-Habituated.[4]

Most of our so-called reasoning consists of finding arguments for going on believing as we already do.

-James Harvey Robinson

Let me state from the outset that when I suggest that conflict is an expected part of any marriage, I am not in any way suggesting that couples become habituated to conflict. I would not want any couple to take what I am saying as encouragement to resign themselves to a steady stream of conflict in their marriage.

Quite honestly, people who end up in a Conflict-Habituated marriage are often "argumentative types," people who tend to get a rush by arguing and debating their position. Sometimes it's argument for argument's sake (just for the fun of it), and sometimes it's the thrill of defeating someone else and crushing their point of view, but in the end, such individuals do not engage in conflict with the intent of rational and reasonable resolution of disagreements. Such an approach to conflict is not healthy for a marriage.[5]

But for most of us men, this is not the primary problem we face when it comes to conflict in our marriage. Few of us get a rush from conflict with our wives. Few of us see marital disagreements as some sort of sport to be enjoyed for its own sake. For the vast majority of us, the problem is actually just the opposite—few of us see our wives as a sparring partner for our argumentative urges, but rather, most of us are inclined to avoid as much conflict with her as we can.[6]

The Demand-Withdraw Pattern

This may at first glance seem to be a reasonable response on our part, but a problem frequently emerges. As we avoid these confrontations that are a normal and necessary part of a healthy marriage, our wives will typically begin to intensify their efforts to discuss those things that are of concern to them. And their subsequent justification (sometimes articulated out loud) might sound something like this: "If only you would listen to me, then I wouldn't have to be such a raving maniac to get my point across." And for many of us men, our response (almost never articulated out loud) might come along these lines: "Every time we talk, I feel like you're trying to back me into a corner, and I'm not going to go there."

ॐ

We often hear we have a battle of the sexes when, in fact, we have a war in which only one side has shown up. Most men put their heads into the sand and hope the bullets will miss.

-Warren Farrell

This tendency to avoid conflict with our wives and their increasing insistence that they be heard is so prevalent that a term has been created to quickly and easily describe it—the Demand–Withdraw Pattern of marital interaction.[7] In over 80% of marriages it is the wife who consistently brings up issues about the marriage, and it is the husband who consistently attempts to put off discussions of those issues.[8]

ॐ

The calmest husbands make the stormiest wives.

-Isaac d'Israeli

Furthermore, as this Demand–Withdraw Pattern persists, then the negative consequences in the marriage can be exacerbated by what one author referred to as "the harsh start-up"— wives who out of frustration begin discussions with their husbands more forcefully than they intend (and more directly than their husbands appreciate). Such harsh start-ups typically intensify the withdrawal response by men.[9]

Simply Wanting To Be Heard

Admittedly, it is one thing to be able to name something, and it is quite another to experience it. Actually living this Demand–Withdraw Pattern in your marriage and experiencing the harsh start-up from your wife is far more difficult than merely reading about it somewhere in a book. When our wives regularly bring up concerns about our marriage, we can end up feeling badgered, nagged, and criticized. We can end up wondering, "Where's the love?" And when we regularly avoid such discussions, our wives can end up feeling frustrated and hurt, wondering, "If he loves me, why isn't he as interested in our marriage as I am?"

> ᭡
> *Of all the sure-fire infernal devices ever invented by all the devils in hell for destroying love, nagging is the deadliest. It never fails. Like the bite of the king cobra, it always destroys, always kills.*
>
> -Dale Carnegie

As men, we can struggle to understand how there can be so many things wrong that we have to talk about them so of-ten—after all, if it's not a problem, then why does it need to be discussed? We can struggle to figure out how to get some of these things fixed so that we won't have to talk about them over and over again—after all, don't these things work like fixing a toilet: once it's fixed, then you don't have to worry about it any more? And we can struggle with what often comes across as criticism—after all, if she sees so many problem ar-eas in our marriage and she expresses them so forcefully, isn't she really saying that the problem is me?

But the reality in most marriages is that our wives do not want to nag us or browbeat us or criticize us. They simply want to be heard. As women, our wives are far more sensitive to marriage and family issues than are we men. And as is true in virtually every context—whether it be the sports fanatic or the political activist or the weather enthusiast or the gear head—we are *all* inclined to initiate discussions of those top-ics to which we are most sensitive.

Therefore, it stands to reason that our wives would more frequently bring up such topics for discussion. And very often they are not looking for immediate changes or quick solutions or fool-proof answers from us. They are looking to be heard. They want to know that we are listening and that their concerns have been taken seriously. They want to know that we are as interested in our life together as they are.[10]

> ৺
>
> *If you don't understand, they feel frustrated. If you don't try to understand, they feel hurt.*
>
> -Mark Goulston

All I Wanted Was For Someone To Hear Me

I have a colleague named Marty who gained some key insights into his wife and into his marriage (as well as into himself) one day last fall. It was early October when Marty had scheduled appointments on the same day with his supervisor at work, with his doctor at the clinic, and with the auto tech at the car dealership. With each of these individuals, Marty tried to carefully articulate the concerns he was having—the work environment in his department, about his physical health, and about how poorly his new car was running—and in each situation Marty received what he described as "mere lip service."

Marty elaborated on his experience this way: "Here I was, going to each of these people with legitimate concerns, things that were bothering me, issues that I cared about. And I ended up feeling like none of them wanted to give me the time of day. I felt like they blew off my concerns like spit in the wind. If any of them listened to me at all (which I seriously doubt), their listening didn't translate at all into any sort of expressed interest in the concerns that I brought to them.

"All I wanted was for someone to hear me, to acknowledge my concerns, and to show that they were willing to work with me on some constructive solutions. But all I got was lip service. By the end of the day I was so angry that the guy at the auto dealership really got the brunt of my frustration. I didn't do anything stupid, like throw something, but I certainly got his attention. When he barely looked up from the computer screen long enough to tell me that "they couldn't find anything wrong" with my car and to "bring it back another time" if I wanted to, I made it very clear that I was angry and that I was going to get some satisfaction and I was going to get it *now*. I didn't want to be such a raving maniac, but I didn't feel like I had any other choice."

Forcefulness: An Understandable Response?

It was at this point that Marty's tone of voice changed as he began to talk about his marriage. "I don't know how much we've ever talked about my marriage with Sue," Marty related, "but let me quickly summarize it by saying that up until that day last fall, it had become pretty rocky. Sue has always been one to speak her mind, and early in our marriage I tried to sort of placate her when she would raise concerns about our marriage or about me. I would try to reassure her and make her feel better, but I seldom responded to her in any real concrete way. It just seemed so much easier to quell the immediate storm and then try to avoid the next one for as long as possible.

Withdrawers must be reeled in as smoothly, firmly, and gently as a big fish. Hostile efforts to pursue a partner who is hiding just make the distancer dig in deeper.

-Frank Pittman

"This seemed to work for a while, but Sue gradually became more and more forceful in what she had to say. And the amount of time it took her to get up a full head of steam got less and less, until eventually she could get really worked up right from the start of nearly every conversation. 'Honey, we need to talk!' she'd state matter of factly, and then she'd really let me have it. And needless to say, as Sue became more persistent in raising her concerns and I became more persistent in avoiding them, a lot of the warmth and closeness between us got worn away. Up until that day last fall, I had blamed Sue for all this, and I had pretty much concluded that I had unwittingly married a nag.

"But after my experience with my supervisor at work and then the doctor and then the car dealership, I began to wonder whether this is the way Sue was feeling in our marriage. Did she feel like she came to me with legitimate concerns, only to have me dismiss them as insignificant (if I discussed them at all)? I was so frustrated that day last fall that I felt I had to get more and more demanding if there was any hope of being heard. Is this what Sue had been feeling—that if she didn't say things forcefully, then she just wouldn't be heard? I began to wonder if maybe I was more at fault in my marriage than I had thought—maybe Sue's nagging was an understandable response to not being listened to."

Not A Nag After All

Marty went on to describe how in the wake of that fortuitous day last fall, he began to engage his wife's concerns. Although it was difficult for Marty and Sue to change a pattern of relating that had been built up over their seven years of marriage, Marty was determined not to respond to Sue in the way he had personally been treated that day last fall. He was determined to take her concerns seriously and to not simply attempt to placate her. He also worked very hard at not avoiding the inevitable conflicts that emerged in their marriage.

Being heard is so close to being loved that for the average person, they are almost indistinguishable.

-David Augsburger

Marty put it this way: "I began to listen to Sue and to respond to what was bothering her. Regardless of whether she wants to talk about the things she sees that aren't working right or the things that could be better or the things I need to take care of or the ways in which I could change, I hear her. We don't always agree, but we do talk things out now.

"And I am happy to report that I did not marry a nag after all. I just married a woman who wanted to be heard, a woman who wanted to know that I was interested in what was important to her, a woman who wanted me to care about our life together as much as she did. And you know, I've found out that she has some good insights into how our marriage can become more of what both of us have wanted.

"Although I never thought it would work this way, the warmth and closeness between us has returned, and it is deeper and richer than it ever was before. I still don't enjoy some of the conflict between Sue and me, but I have come to see that it is an important part of our life together. Because we are working to constructively resolve our differences, we are actually growing closer. This is what I wanted all along—I certainly didn't marry Sue so that we could become more distant from each other—but I just never figured that conflict was a vital part of the process that would facilitate the closeness that I desired."

Are You A Fortunate Man?

There is a growing body of research evidence confirming what Marty experienced first hand. When we attempt to avoid conflict with our wives, there are predictably deleterious consequences for our marriages.[11] As one marriage expert put it: "The most important advice I can give to men who want their marriages to work is… *not* to avoid. Sidestepping a problem won't make it go away—on the contrary, leaving the conflict unresolved will just upset your wife more. Realize that she needs to talk about what's eating at her to keep the relationship working smoothly. Unpleasant though it may be for you, by venting her feelings she is working to keep your marriage healthy…. This doesn't mean that you have to 'give in' to all of your wife's criticisms. But you should always respect her opinion and try to understand what she's saying rather than reacting like you're on automatic pilot."[12]

If you, like Marty, have a wife who is invested in you and in your marriage and she lets you know what is on her mind, then you are a fortunate man.[13] Admittedly, most of us have not thought about it in this way—that we are actually fortunate to have a wife who freely

The RealAge web site recommends finding a "reminder buddy" to improve your health, one with whom to exercise, eat right, etc. "Reminder Buddy"—such a nice term for the role of a spouse, sounds so much better than "nagging."

-Diane Sollee

Some of us are like Wheelbarrows—only useful when pushed, and very easily upset.

-Jack Herbert

brings up her concerns—but this is the truth of the situation. In a culture like ours, a culture in which marriage success is so dependent on the establishment of mutual affection, companionship, and unity (a sense of we-ness between husbands and wives), the type of sensitivity to relationships that our wives bring into the marriage is a great asset. Research findings have made it clear—the husband who engages the concerns of his wife and actively listens to what she has to say is far more likely to have a thriving marriage.[14] As one noted marriage researcher put it: "Time and again we can separate the happy from the unstable couples based on whether the husband is willing to accept influence from his wife.... Men who are willing to accept influence are happily married. Those who are not see their marriages become unstable."[15]

Rules To Love By

Do not avoid conflict with your wife.

There is possibly no task in marriage that is more difficult for us than engaging in constructive conflict with our wives. What we want is greater closeness, and it seems so counter-productive to argue with the person with whom we want to experience greater connection. Furthermore, for some of us, marital conflict is actually a physically unsettling experience.[16]

But nonetheless, if we really do value our marriages and we want them to thrive, then we cannot avoid conflict with the woman we love. She wants to know that we care as much about the marriage as she does, and consistently hearing her out is one vital way to let her know that this is true.

Making Time To Talk

In his insightful little book titled *The Screwtape Letters*, C. S. Lewis describes how a senior devil (Screwtape) instructs a junior devil in the art of leading men and women astray from those things that are most valuable and most important in their lives. One of the first things Screwtape mentions is the seductive busyness of life. In the midst of a hectic and frenzied lifestyle around which so much of modern life revolves, those things most precious to us can be overlooked as we give our attention to those things that are most pressing. In trying to meet all the demands of modern life, it is not unusual to find many couples gradually giving less and less attention to the person (and the relationship) that is most important. As Screwtape suggests, when people become busy with many things, they are less attentive to those that are most important. We don't even notice that we are beginning to grow apart from the one we love.

The antidote? Set aside time every week simply to talk. And if you are anything like most couples, you are going to have to put it into your schedule. Most couples find that they have to literally pull out their calendars every week and find a chunk of time (at least an hour) where nothing else will happen except conversation. Otherwise, other commitments keep getting in the way, and the conversations that are needed simply don't happen. And many couples find that in order to accomplish this feat—communicating with no interruptions or distractions for at least an hour—they need to get away from all the commotion and the demands that are so commonly found at home.

Love must be nurtured. First and foremost, it demands time. We often encourage busy couples to schedule time together or no-television nights at home. Heart-to-heart talks don't happen on the go.

-Les and Leslie Parrott

Years ago—based on the wise advice of someone we trusted—my wife and I began to go out once a week simply to talk. This was not a date night nor

John Buri

was it a time to go out and enjoy a sporting event together, this was simply one time per week when there were no anticipated distractions, interruptions, or obligations. A time when we were committed to giving each other our full and undivided attention.

I don't think we have missed a week for many years now. It has become a highly valued time—a time when we know that we can talk about anything and everything, a time without which many topics would have received nothing more than leftover moments from the busyness of our lives. Quite honestly, these weekly times of discussion proved to be a major springboard for the changes we needed to implement in our relationship if our marriage was to ever move in the direction of what we had hoped for on our wedding day. It was only a matter of time before we began to experience first-hand what several marriage therapists have strongly encouraged— for the good of your marriage, make time to talk every week.[17]

Quirks And Idiosyncrasies

One of the things that I have found helpful to couples as they sort through the inevitable conflicts in their marriage is to encourage them to break down their arguments into three categories of disagreement. The first of these sources of conflict are those quirky behaviors and idiosyncratic habits that we all have and we all naturally take with us into our marriages. Whether it be the loud sneeze in public or the slurping of soup or the little whistle when we breathe through the nose or the slouching posture or the sloppy eating, these quirks can be a source of irritation to married couples. It is the rare individual who lives in a marriage where there are no quirky little spousal behaviors that are a source of irritation.

> Never, never did we marry just the piece of a human being—even though it's only bits and pieces we see before the marriage. We marry the other one whole. But always we buy the package before we can open it.
>
> -Walter Wangerin, Jr

When such irritating idiosyncrasies are the source of disagreement in a marriage, then loving tolerance is the antidote. Without developing a patient acceptance of such behaviors, then those things that are really just minor imperfections can become major sources of criticism—"Do you have to sneeze so loudly in public, it's embarrassing!" "Do you have to slurp when you eat? It's irritating!" "Do you have to whistle when you breathe? Can't you wear a nose strip or something?" "Why don't you stand up straight, you remind me of a baboon!" "Can't you eat without spilling, your place always looks like a two year old was sitting there!" And needless to say, such criticism will end up undermining even the most ardently professed love— warmth and closeness is difficult to maintain in a relationship that is riddled by criticism.[18]

I have a friend whose wife died when he was forty. I was talking with him one day after working out, and he told me, "You know, John, when Mary Jean was alive it was so irritating when she laughed. She had one of those loud, shrill laughs—almost like listening to a hyena. Unfortunately, I had a heart the size of a pea when Mary Jean was alive. I would actually get so annoyed when she laughed that I let it get in the way of my love for her. I have to tell you, I would give anything to be able to hear that laugh one more time."

The way to love anything is to realize that it might be lost.

-G. K. Chesterton

Personal Preferences

The second category of disagreement that married couples need to negotiate is the domain of personal preferences. We all have some of these. We prefer that the toothpaste be squeezed from the bottom of the tube. We prefer that there not be any crumbs left in the butter container. We prefer that the dishes be washed before relaxing for the evening. We prefer that the toilet lid be put down after each use. We prefer to eat dinner earlier rather than later. We prefer that the bed be made each morning and that clothes not be left out in the bedroom. And the list goes on…. I am sure that each of us can add numerous examples here!

The number of personal preferences that we bring with us into our marriages can be virtually endless, and these personal preferences can in and of themselves be a significant source of conflict between spouses. But one thing that is almost certain to heighten the intensity of conflict over what amounts to mere preferences is when one spouse insists that what he or she prefers represents the way things *ought to be*.

Take for example the following comments. "*Everybody* knows that you are *supposed to* squeeze the toothpaste from the bottom of the tube!" "*No considerate person* would ever leave crumbs in the butter!" "I don't know any *right-thinking person* who leaves their dishes until the next day!" "Toilet seats are *supposed to be* lowered; that's what they're there for!" "Dinners were *meant to be* eaten no later than 6:00!" "I can't imagine *any reasonable people* leaving their bed unmade and their clothes laying around."

>
> *Marriage is like a flourishing garden, alive with soil, colorful blooms, delightful fragrances and pleasant surprises—and thorns, beetles, weeds, and perhaps a mole.*
>
> -Nancy McCord

Who Put You In Charge?

When mere personal preferences are elevated to the status of oughts, differences of opinion are almost certain to be blown out of proportion. When this happens, it's not unusual to witness reactions of this sort: "Who's to say that this is how it ought to be done?" "Who put you in charge of determining what's right?" "Just because you feel that this is the way things should be done doesn't necessarily make it so!"

> *It is better to debate a question without settling it than to settle a question without debating it.*
>
> -Joseph Joubert

There are some marriages where disagreements over personal preferences are rare, but this is most often the case when one partner is excessively acquiescent to the desires of his or her spouse. The desire to simply please that spouse is so strong that he or she seldom expresses (much less argues for) his or her own preferences. Unfortunately, while such marriages may offer an appearance of peace and stability, they often result in a build up of resentments in the acquiescent partner, and these resentments can slowly have an eroding effect upon the love in the marriage.[19]

If we want successful marriages, then we need to place our likes and dislikes where they belong—out in the open *and* at the level of personal preferences. This does not mean that these preferences are insignificant. On the contrary, they can often be pretty weighty issues in a marriage. But rather, this simply means that they should not receive the force of emphasis that typically comes with an "ought" or a "should" or a "must." Instead, we need to learn how to clearly express our personal preferences—listening to one another, talking through the origins of these preferences, and understanding the strength and importance of each person's preferences. And in the end, our ability to communicate, to negotiate, and to compromise with one another about these personal preferences will go a long way toward building a happy marriage.[18]

> *The success of marriage comes not in finding the "right" person, but in the ability of both partners to adjust to the real person they inevitably realize they married.*
>
> -John Fischer

Resolving Personal Preference Issues[9]

Admittedly, personal preferences can be an annoyance, but they are not inherently destructive; how we deal with them may be, but the fact that we have them is not. And as many of us have discovered, working through our personal preference differences is a lot like weeding a garden—not the most pleasant of activities, but one that nonetheless has to be done (sometimes over and over again).[20]

> *We have not really budged a step until we take up residence in someone else's point of view.*
>
> -John Erskine

I would like to offer a rule of thumb that I use when helping couples resolve their personal preference issues. It is a fairly simple principle. It goes like this. If the particular issue you're wrestling with is one where compromise is possible, then pursue a reasonable compromise. For example, one couple I worked with had a huge argument over squeezing the toothpaste—do you always squeeze it from the bottom or is it okay to squeeze from the middle? They came up with a compromise—they each use a separate tube of toothpaste.

Sometimes, however, it isn't possible to come up with a solution in which both individuals can get their way. Case in point: one couple enjoyed entertaining, but they had an ongoing disagreement about when to clean up. She wanted to clean up before they went to bed, whereas he wanted to take care of things in the morning. Obviously, they couldn't both get their way—unless he simply went to bed and let his wife clean everything up by herself. (Not a good idea!) I encouraged them to talk through this issue with one principle in mind. Who stands to lose the most by not having things done in the way that each would prefer? For this particular couple, she found it difficult to sleep if she knew that the house was a mess. He, on the other hand, simply preferred to do it in the morning. They now always make sure that the house is clean before they go to bed

Beyond Quirks And Personal Preferences

As troubling as the conflict from individual quirks and personal preferences can be in marital unions, there is a third category of disagreement that is often far more problematic than is either of these sources of conflict. We are talking here about those irresponsible and destructive behavior patterns that have deleterious consequences for the individual as well as for the spouse.

For example, when we bring our addictions into the marriage with us

> *If we take people as they are, we make them worse. If we treat them as if they were what they ought to be, we help them become what they are capable of becoming.*
>
> -Johann von Goethe

(whether they be addictions to alcohol, sex, gambling, food, drugs, pornography), our behaviors will inevitably have adverse consequences for ourselves as well as for our marriage. When we repeatedly exhibit anger, deception, cheating, arrogance, or stealing, we might argue that these are issues of personal preference, but they are not. Their consequences are far too destructive to be mere issues of preference. They undermine not only the integrity of the individual, but also the integrity of the marriage. When we have persistent problems with poor impulse control, or hypersensitivity to correction, or television mesmerism at the expense of the family, or excessive preoccupation with work, we are not talking about little idiosyncrasies that need to be overlooked. We are taking about behavior patterns that seriously weaken the bonds of the marriage vows.

The Marriage Crucible

Marriage has been likened to a crucible, a container that is used to purify metals. As the heat beneath the crucible increases to greater and greater intensity, the imperfections in the metal rise to the surface and it is there that they can be recognized for what they are and removed, and gradually the metal is purified.

> *Of all knowledge, the wise and good seek most to know themselves.*
>
> -William Shakespeare

For many of us, the analogy here is an obvious one. There is nothing we will ever do that will produce quite as much heat in our lives as being married (except maybe when we add children to the mix), and it is in this context that some of our greatest weaknesses get exposed.[21]

When I entered my marriage as a young man, I had what some might refer to as "anger issues"—there were particular circumstances in my life to which I could respond with fairly strong outbursts of anger. These bouts with anger had not been at all apparent to my wife (even through five years of dating), and they had only been vaguely apparent to me. But once exposed to the heat of married life, my issues with anger quickly became obvious.

I will never forget the shock on my wife's face the first time I angrily grabbed the car keys and stormed out of the apartment. I tried to argue that this was just one of those little quirks about me that she was going to have to get used to. I tried to convince her that this was just my preferred way of dealing with the stress in my life. But in actuality, this was a destructive behavior pattern that almost cost me my marriage.

Responsibility For One Another

The reality is that when we marry, we agree to take on a certain level of responsibility *to* one another and *for* one another. We throw in our lots together ("for better or for worse") not knowing for sure what will emerge in the heat of the crucible of married life. Little did my wife suspect that some of "the worse" was going to involve such intense displays of anger.

But the marriage promise entails a commitment that we will not simply wallow in our unhealthy, destructive behavior patterns nor will we glibly overlook such behaviors in our partner. Instead, healthy marriages

> *He who stops being better stops being good.*
>
> -Oliver Cromwell

operate as a mutual change process—while there is an appreciation for all that is good in the partner and in the marriage, there is also a tacit agreement to identify and to work at eliminating those unhealthy, irresponsible, destructive behaviors that do harm to us, to our partner, and to the marriage.

> *It is a lovely thing to have a husband and wife developing together. That is what marriage really means: helping one another to reach full status of being persons, responsible... beings who do not run away from life.*
>
> -Paul Tournie

Such an approach of mutual accountability by husbands and wives is a key element of enduring, successful marriages. Couples who have experienced a lasting love for their spouse and a genuine satisfaction with their marriage have had this in common—they have embraced a mutual responsibility for one another as well as for their marriage. Consistently these couples have reported that because of their spouses and for the sake of their marriages, they have changed for the better—objectively speaking, they have become more healthy human beings.[23] As one man told me: "The best thing I ever did was to say 'I do;' not because it made my life easier but because it made me a better person. And I am grateful to my wife for the huge part she had to play in that process."

We are shaped and fashioned by what we love.
-Johann von Goethe

The authors of the book titled *The Good Marriage: How and Why Love Lasts* researched "the secrets" of couples who managed to nourish their love and appreciation for one another over several years of marriage. They offered the following summary statement of one of these secrets: "A good marriage…is transformative… men and women come to adulthood unfinished, and over the course of a marriage they change each other profoundly."[23] In all marriages that not only survive, but also thrive, spouses help each other change for the better.

Not What I Want, But What We Need

We have here been discussing the three main categories of conflict in marriages: our quirks and idiosyncrasies, our personal preferences, and our unhealthy, destructive behavior patterns. This may at first glance seem fairly straightforward, but any couple who has attempted to separate their marital disagreements into these three categories will attest to the fact that this is not as easy as it may at first appear.

Marriage alone does not make you a better person, but accepting its challenges does.
- Linda & Charlie Bloom

For example, individuals who are fairly intolerant may find it difficult to graciously overlook those little irritating behavioral quirks emanating from their spouse. Those who are fairly accustomed to getting their own way may struggle when asked to let go of a relatively insignificant personal preference. Those who believe that their way is *the right way* may insist that mere personal preferences are instances of unhealthy behaviors. And those who do not want to change their destructive behavior patterns may argue that they are merely issues of personal preference.

There is no easy way around it. As individuals who come into marriage with different backgrounds, different experiences, different expectations, and different ways of thinking, it stands to reason that we will have some differences of opinion as to what constitutes an idiosyncrasy versus a personal preference versus an objectively unhealthy behavior pattern. These differences of opinion are inevitable and understandable, but over time reasonable people can work through these differences. Sometimes it may be necessary to agree to disagree for a time—but always with an agreement to revisit the discussion (many times, if necessary). Sometimes it may require the help of outside resources—a close trusted friend, a pastor, a counselor.But people of honesty and integrity can resolve these differences.

> *Honest disagreement is often a good sign of progress.*
> -Mahatma Gandhi

Rules To Love By

People who understand that marriage entails a mutual responsibility for one another and for their life together can work through their disagreements—for such individuals, conflicts are not so much about *what I want* as they are about *what we need.*

And in the end, the effort expended is well worth it—knowing which behaviors need to be lovingly accepted, which ones need to be negotiated and compromised, and which ones need to be changed gives a couple a valuable framework for enduring marital love.

The Encroachment Of Criticism

In the midst of conflict, there is one pitfall to which even the most well-intentioned couples are vulnerable. This pitfall is arguably the most destructive act (short of infidelity) that an individual can thrust on his or her spouse—this is the pitfall of criticism. If you want to kill your marriage with a single blow, cheat; but if you want to slowly bludgeon it to death, be critical. Any couple who hopes to maintain a disposition of love in their relationship has to be ready to do battle with the encroachment of criticism into their marriage.

There is little in life that can't be said politely, even lovingly.

-Frank Pittman

Take, for example, an instance in which there is a need to talk with your spouse about the fact that the lights were left on *again* in several rooms of the house. When you have this discussion, make sure that you keep it centered on the facts—several lights were left on. Unfortunately, out of frustration, couples can sometimes slip into one-liners— how "careless, lazy, or wasteful"

The cheap thrill you get from putting down your partner isn't so cheap.

-Linda and Charlie Bloom

John Buri

their spouse is—and when this happens, criticism threatens to erode the sense that the two of them are a team. In instances such as these, it would be good to ask ourselves: Does the expense of a few lights left on (or even many lights left on) justify the damage to the partner and to the love in the marriage that is accomplished through criticism?

Or imagine that you climb into the car and find the gas gauge on empty *again*. Work to keep the ensuing discussion on the fact that the car was out of gas and therefore your morning commute was far more hectic than you had anticipated. Don't allow the conversation to slip into put-downs—how "thoughtless, rude, or inconsiderate" your spouse is. The quicksand of criticism has sucked the love out of many a marriage, and if you allow your personal inconvenience to be expressed through criticism, then yours will be among them.

Or consider the case in which you need to talk about the fact that because of excessive spending, there is *again* more month than money left in the family budget. When you have the necessary discussion, keep it focused on the budget and what can reasonably be done to either curb

Trust takes years to establish and moments to destroy.

- Linda & Charlie Bloom

spending or to increase income. If you allow the discussion to degenerate into name-calling—how "negligent, senseless, or self-centered" your spouse is—then you have stepped onto the slippery slope of criticism, and your marriage will pay the price. Such name-calling may influence a change in spending habits, but if this is accomplished in a way that destroys marital love, then one has to wonder whether it is worth the cost.

The bottom line is this: Criticism may afford us opportunities to get out our frustrations or to vent our inconveniences

The weak can never forgive. Forgiveness is the attribute of the strong.

-Mahatma Gandhi

or sometimes even to win arguments, but whatever the apparent benefits of criticism, they will always be realized at the expense of our spouse and our marriage.[24]

Rules To Love By

First of all, initiate an agreement between you and your wife that each of you is committed to eliminating criticism in your marriage. This does not mean that you stop expressing your needs or that you stop discussing those things that you would like to see changed in the marriage. It simply means that you will not insult or attack your spouse in the process.

As part of this agreement, reassure one another that you will not only work at eliminating your own use of criticism, but that you will also help your spouse to see when he or she has slipped into a criticizing way of communicating.

Secondly, once this agreement between you and your wife has been established, when you make a mistake (that's *when*, not *if*) and you inadvertently cast a critical remark in the direction of your wife, be quick to apologize. A sincere apology along with an honest desire and effort to change can be incredibly healing to a wounded spouse and to a fractured marriage.[25]

The Need To Grow Up

What I have to say here is not very touchy-feely and it's not loaded with a lot of psychobabble, but it is nonetheless true. When it comes to dealing with conflict in a healthy way in our marriages, for many of us what we need more than anything else is to grow up.

If you think about it very long, you begin to realize that some of the most common pitfalls in resolving marital conflict—avoiding difficult discussions, insisting on having

> ❦
>
> *It's no mistake that "maturity" and "matrimony" come from the same word.*
>
> -Les & Leslie Parrot

things my way, and the use of criticism—are actually the common behavior patterns of children and adolescents. How often have you witnessed children trying to escape a tough conversation—even down to the infant avoiding eye contact? How often have you seen parents asserting with their children (sometimes in the face of pouting and temper tantrums) that what you want frequently needs to be set aside for the sake of the common good? How often have you seen the weapons of criticism—sarcasm, insults, anger, silence—wielded by adolescents in the midst of disagreement?

ॐ

It's not the differences between partners that cause problems, but how the differences are handled when they arise.

- Clifford Notarius & Howard Markman

These sorts of behaviors are standard fare for children and adolescents. But as adults, if we want enduring affection to be the foundation of our marriage, then we are going to have to rise above these more adolescent ways of responding to conflict. Simply put, we are going to have to grow up. Maybe the change process described by a friend of mine will be useful. He referred to it as his four-step process. In his words, "Step 1: I was determined to be more rational and reasonable when conflict arose between my wife and me. Step 2: I acted on my determination. I listened more and reacted less. I gave my wife time to present her point of view. I worked hard at not getting defensive, and to talk things through calmly. Step 3: I listened to myself and I took careful note of my successes--and my failures. Step 4: I repeated step 1, 2, and 3." As a colleague of mine is wont to say: "Growing older happens naturally, but growing up is a matter of choice."

SENSIBLE EFFORT
BY REASONABLE PEOPLE

Healthy conflict resolution is admittedly one of the most difficult (and most important) skill sets to be developed by any couple who desires lasting marital love. But like any skill, it can be learned.

- Avoid the 5 Deadly "Ds" of Disputation—don't be
  - Dictatorial
  - Defensive
  - Demeaning
  - Disrespectful
  - Disregarding

  It is possible to disagree without being disagreeable

- Set aside time each week to talk through issues
  - This is a time to talk about those things that are bothering either of you
  - Find a time each week that works for you as a couple—put that time in your schedule and protect it
  - Find a place that works for you—a place that is without distractions and free of competing demands

- Refuse to fight dirty
  - Don't emphasize a point with fist pounding or door slamming
  - Don't drag past failures, previous disappointments, and lingering grudges into the discussion
  - Don't use threats or ultimatums
  - Don't taunt, mock, sneer, insult, or accuse
  - Don't go silent, refusing to participate in a discussion

- Use active listening
    o Begin with problem discussion, not problem solution
    o The goal of problem discussion is understanding, not agreement
    o Clearly identify the problem to be discussed
    o Focus on one problem at a time
    o Allow your spouse a full hearing
    o No interrupting, no quickly jumping to your point of view, no retaliatory arguments
    o Before presenting your perspective on a problem, demonstrate that you have heard your spouse
    o Paraphrase and summarize what has been said

- And in the end
    o Agree to work as a team
    o See each problem as something the two of you share
    o Never lose sight of the fact that the goal of conflict is not to win, but to work together for the common good
    o Take as your marriage mantra: As for me, we comes first

CHAPTER #6

The Heart Of Intimacy: Communication

You Just Don't Seem To Care

A former student of mine, a pre-med major named Bill, came to see me shortly after becoming engaged at the age of 30. Bill had previously been married (to his high school sweetheart), but their marriage had lasted less than three years. Now as he faced the prospect of his second marriage in less than eight years, he was worried lest this new marriage end up in the same plight as his first one.

The first duty of love is to listen.

-Paul Tillich

What triggered Bill's visit to my office was that his fiancée, Alicia, had started to complain that he didn't really seem to care about those things that were of interest to her. Bill expressed Alicia's concerns about their relationship this way: "She just doesn't think that I am very invested in those things that are important to her. She keeps saying that she just doesn't see many indications from me that I am interested in those things that she cares about. She keeps using terms like 'indifferent,' 'inattentive,' and 'unresponsive.' I'm afraid that if I don't figure out what she's talking about, then she may call off the wedding, and quite honestly, I love her and I don't want to lose her."

Do you Care?

As I sat in my office listening to Bill, some obvious questions kept bouncing back and forth in my mind. Fortunately, my experience with Bill as a former student in three classes provided the type of relationship where I was pretty sure that I could put these questions to him fairly directly, so I asked him: "Bill, is Alicia right? *Do you care? Are you really interested* in those things that seem to be most important to her—the responsibilities and activities that occupy most hours of her day, the things that she really wants to talk about?"

> ❦
>
> *Before marriage, a man declares that he would lay down his life to serve you; after marriage, he won't even lay down his newspaper to talk to you.*
>
> -Helen Rowland

Bill sat quietly for what felt like a very long time before he began to talk in a tone of voice that was half admission of failure and half justification of fact. "To be very honest," he said, "I am not really interested in a lot of the things that Alicia cares about. When we talk, I try to listen and I try to be interested in where she goes and what she spends her time doing, but it often doesn't work very well. I guess a lot of this stuff I just don't care about all that much. And in some ways, I'm not sure why I should. It's not really my stuff—it's about her job, her friends, her hobbies, her book reading club, her insights, her family. And sometimes it seems like she just wants to go on and on about these things, and I'm just not that intrigued by it all. In some ways, this feels like déjà vu all over again—I went through a lot of the same stuff in my first marriage. But I guess I've been hoping that the fact I love Alicia more than I did my wife will get us through this stuff."

The Opposite Of Love Is Indifference

What Bill and I proceeded to talk about caught him by surprise. What Bill had failed to realize (and what many of us men have failed to grasp very well) is the fact that the opposite of love is not hate. Rather, the opposite of love is indifference.[1]

Basically, if a man loves his wife and something is important to her, then it should be important to him as well. For any of us to say "I love you" and then to be indifferent to what is important to our wives is worse than an oxymoron. It may be a difficult reality to face, but it is nonetheless true—every act of indifference shouts loudly in a marriage: "I don't love you enough to care about what matters to you!"

Sometimes it is in our discussions that this destructive indifference leaves its unpleasant residue. As one woman put it: "I just don't feel like he cares. A lot of the time I have to badger him just to sit down and talk with me, and then when we do talk, he seems so distant and disinterested that I just end up walking away feeling hurt and unloved. If he really loves me, wouldn't he want to talk with me about what's on my mind?"

Sometimes the deleterious effects of this indifference can be seen in our many daily household tasks. As one wife said to me: "I don't get it. He knows that I hate it when he leaves his wet towel on the bed and his dirty dishes in the sink, but he still keeps doing it. I feel like a motel maid. If he loved me, wouldn't it matter more to him since he knows it's so important to me?"

> 𝕍
> *Listening is not merely not talking, though even that is beyond most of our powers; it means taking a vigorous, human interest in what is being said.*
> -Alice Duer Miller

And sometimes this indifference rears its ugly head in the daily events of married life. One woman expressed it this way: "I try to know each morning as we walk out the door what he has going on that day—what's on his plate. And then I always want to know in the evening how things went. I love him and I care about the things going on in his life. You'd think he would take at least a little interest in the stuff I have going on each day, but he just doesn't seem to care. He hardly ever asks me what's happening in my day or how things have gone. Doesn't he love me enough to care?"

SENSIBLE EFFORT
BY REASONABLE PEOPLE

Taking an active interest is actually a very simple process. It involves asking questions. It involves listening. It involves talking. Basically, it involves caring.

- Do you know those things that weigh most heavily on your wife's mind?
    o About her work?
    o About her friends?
    o About household tasks?
    o About her family?
    o About your marriage?
    o About herself?

- Are you aware of the most important events in your wife's day?
    o Before they happen, what they are? Why they are important to her?
    o After they have happened, how they went? What effect they have had on her?

Each member of the couple must be aware of what is going on in the mind of the other. You don't do that with most people in your life. You don't need to—many personal things you just keep to yourself. But in a relationship as close as marriage, you are living a shared life; and if you don't know what the other person is feeling, thinking, and planning, you'll soon be in trouble.

-David & Vera Mace

- **Do you know those things that have brought your wife her greatest joys? Her greatest disappointments?**
    - **In the last week?**
    - **In the last month?**
    - **In the last year?**

- **Are you aware of those things that your wife most hopes for? Those things that she most fears?**
    - **About her career?**
    - **About the many responsibilities she carries?**
    - **About her relationships?**
    - **About her health?**
    - **About her physical attractiveness?**
    - **About her family?**
    - **About her life with you?**

The Message Of Indifference Is Clear

As much as we may at times not want to admit it, the message of indifference is clear. We marry planning to be central to our spouse's world, but indifference makes it clear that we are not. We marry knowing full well that some of life's struggles await us, but indifference tells us that we face them largely on our own. We marry anticipating that we will be appreciated and valued in our partner's life, but indifference signals a very different reality, one of being unappreciated and devalued. We marry with the intent of being a team, but indifference makes it obvious that we are primarily going it alone.

The conviction that your partner is on your side is one of the foundations of a long-lasting friendship.

-John M. Gottman

Rules To Love By

Indifference is one of the most destructive routine acts in a marriage.[2] While most of us marry with the intent that we are going to take this journey called life *together*—that whatever comes, we won't be facing it alone—indifference delivers a clear and harshly different message. Like a battering ram, the slow dull thud of indifference will destroy the walls of togetherness in virtually any marriage.

For each of us men, if something is important to our wives, then it should be important to us as well. If she cares, then we should care also. And feigned interest will seldom suffice—most of our wives can spot a fake a mile away.

This doesn't mean that everything of importance to our wives will necessarily carry the same weight for us, but it does mean that our wives need to know that they do not carry these things alone. It means that we will give the time, effort, and attention that is indicative of sincere interest.

Too Much Me Rather Than We

I grew up in an alcoholic home. If you know anything about alcoholic homes, then you know that they tend to be unreliable, unpredictable, and (to some extent) untrustworthy. Simply put, you can't always count on people to be there for you, even if they sincerely want to be. As a result, I learned at a very young age that if I depended on others and allowed myself to get too close, then I was setting myself up for disappointment and hurt.

Now this was not something I intentionally decided to do. It was not something that I was consciously aware of, but over time I simply began to rely less and less on others, and more and more on myself. Essentially, I was operating from the mindset that if you don't get too close and you don't rely on other people too much, then you aren't going to get hurt when they aren't there for you. And this unconscious response to my alcoholic home environment worked well in every area of my life—school, sports, work, male friendships. But then I got married.

I have to confess—if you had asked me on my wedding day, I would have told you that I was a darn good catch. But it wasn't long before Kathy began to express a desire for more closeness between us. She really did want more interdependence—more of me relying on her and her being able to rely on me. She wanted a husband, not a roommate. She had already had lots of roommates in her life—but in our marriage, she wanted more. Reasonably, she wanted two me's actively engaged in the process of becoming a we.

> ঔ
>
> *You don't marry one person, you marry three—the person your think they are, the person they are, and the person they are becoming as the result of being married to you.*
>
> *-Richard Needham*

But Why Change?

I have to admit that I went into my marriage oblivious to the fact that I was so self-sufficient that there was little hope for we-ness to develop between Kathy and me. I did not marry with the desire for a growing disconnection from the woman I loved; after all, she was the best thing that had ever happened to me. But in spite of my good intentions, that is exactly what began to happen. My failure to take a sincere interest in the things she most cared about, and my reluctance to share with her what was going on in my life, made it difficult for us to develop any solid, ongoing foundation for intimacy.

And as Kathy continued to press for greater closeness between us (and less self-sufficiency from me), I began to wrestle with

> ঔ
>
> *Only fools and dead men don't change... Fools won't. Dead men can't.*
>
> *-John H. Patterson*

a crucial question: Why change? I asked myself: Should I change to please my wife? After all, she would be so much happier if I would just become less self-sufficient and start connecting with her more, taking a greater interest in what was going on in her life, and letting her into my life more as well. Added to this soul-searching was the advice (from a friend at my bachelor's party years ago) that kept reverberating back and forth in my mind: "Always remember, John, a happy wife is a happy life."

I suspect that many of you have faced this sort of decision. Your wife has requested a change, and you need to decide whether you should change simply to please her. Further complicating this type of decision may be the suggestion (often implied, but sometimes overtly stated): "If you really loved me, then you'd change simply because I want you to."

Should you change to please your wife? The answer is: No. It doesn't matter how much you love her, changing to please her won't work. Even if some change does happen, it will be forced, half-hearted, and short-lived. Furthermore, changing to please someone else can often produce anger and resentment. It can even result in score-keeping: "I worked on this change for you, so the least you can do for me is to change this thing about you."

This left me with the question: Should I change to please myself? Quite honestly, I was already quite pleased with the way I was. Being fairly guarded and self-sufficient had served me well throughout my life. I really didn't have any desire to change to please myself. I was already quite happy with who I was.

Then why change? The answer was surprisingly obvious once I began to see it. Simply put, I needed to change in order to become a better person. Just because I had

The important thing is this: to be able at any moment to sacrifice what we are for what we could become.

-Linda & Charlie Bloom

become comfortable with my self-sufficient ways of relating to people (even my wife) did not make it any less true that as human beings, we are meant to have a life of connection, a life of inter-dependence, a life of relying on others and having them rely on us—in short, a life of love.[3]

Over the years, I have encouraged hundreds of men (and women) to approach their marriage with an eye to becoming a better human being. As numerous marriage experts have emphasized, if you want a stable and satisfying marriage, then both partners should have a desire to change and to grow (both as individuals and as a couple) throughout their married life together.[4] Admittedly, most of us have found out that it is the rare man who enters marriage void of areas in his life that are in need of change. Fortunately, marriage provides a great opportunity for on-the-job training and on-the-job transformation.

I Thought Intimacy Was Something Sexual

Possibly the greatest challenge facing us men who desire a relationship of closeness and connection with the woman we love is the challenge of intimacy. Numerous authors have expounded at great length on the importance of intimacy in any sincere love relationship, and the fact has been firmly established—if you want a marriage founded on love, then you need to foster

When two hearts are connected, the biggest problems become workable; when they are not, the smallest difficulties seem insurmountable.

-Linda & Charlie Bloom

intimacy between you and your wife.[5]

There is no doubt a lot of confusion surrounding this thing called "intimacy." For example, one day in class we were discussing the topic of intimacy, and one of the young women in the class spoke up: "I just don't understand why men don't want to be intimate. Why don't you want to get close?" At this, a young man in the back of the room blurted out (obviously without thinking first): "We do too want to be intimate, but you girls just don't want to get sexual." Needless to say, the ensuing discussion was a lively one!

Admittedly, there is a closeness that can be engendered through sex, and sex is certainly an important part of marital love.[6] We need to never forget that sex is one thing that differentiates the friendship we have with our wives versus all the other relationships in our lives. But sex is not the type of intimacy we are talking about here. Rather, we are here referring to the intimacy that is based on the closeness that derives from deep personal patterns of communication.

Monster Trucks And Navel Lint

When talking about communication, it is important to acknowledge from the outset that prior to our serious dating relationships, most of us men did not spend a lot of time experiencing (or probably even thinking about) this essential element of successful marriages. As boys, how often did we sit around and "share with our friends" what was going on in our lives? Sure we talked, but what we talked about centered on things like monster trucks, whether or not there are extraterrestrials, and who should be the MVP this season. Most of us men did not sit around and talk about our deepest thoughts (and many of us didn't even know we had deepest thoughts). We did not share with each other anything that might resemble a secret (unless you want to include the secret passage into the local gym). But it is these very types of conversations that women began to experience soon after they began to talk.

Drawing on extensive research, several authors have argued that by the age of five or six, most little girls begin to spend time together simply sitting and talking with each other. They share their thoughts, tell secrets, and exchange confidences day in and day out in the normal course of their play together. The purpose of this type of conversation is to make connections, to establish friendships, and to negotiate relationships. It has been described as "rapport-talk." Little boys, on the other hand, spend much of their talking time imparting information (such as the batting averages of the top ten hitters in baseball), exhibiting knowledge (such as the origins of navel lint) and establishing status (such as their most recent accomplishments). This has been referred to as "report-talk."[7]

Ultimately the bond of all companionship, whether in marriage or in friendship, is conversation.

-Oscar Wilde

Rapport-Talk Versus Report-Talk

It is with these many years of experience doing report-talk rather than rapport-talk that most of us enter marriage. And it should not come as a surprise that the differences in communication patterns deriving from these experiences is a frequent source of consternation among married couples.[8]

One man explained to me his personal experience of the clash between rapport-talk and report-talk in this way: "My wife will ask me what's on my mind, and I don't blow her off like Al Bundy (of *Married With Children*) did when he told Peg, 'If I wanted you to know, I'd be talking instead of thinking.' I try to answer her seriously. I tell her about the projects I have going at work and the things I would like to get done around the house and who is playing in the game that I am looking forward

I think a man and a woman should choose each other for life, for the simple reason that a long life with all its accidents is barely enough time for a man and a woman to understand each other and....to understand is to love.

-William Butler Yeats

to watching this weekend. But she invariably ends up telling me that we just don't communicate with each other. It's frustrating because I really am trying to communicate with her, but oftentimes I'm not quite sure what it is she's looking for."

This man's wife, on the other hand, expressed her frustration this way: "It is sometimes so exasperating. Even if we have talked for over an hour, I can walk away feeling as it we have hardly communicated at all. It's not like I'm disinterested in the projects he has going, but I really want to know *where he's at* in the middle of all those projects, what *he's going through* as he works on all those things. Doesn't he love me enough or trust me enough to talk with me personally, to let me know what's going on with him?"

The truth is, when our conversations are limited to *the things we are doing* (report-talk), then we will experience limited intimacy with the woman we love. Even when these conversations include those things that we have *in common with her*—remodeling projects on the house, or activities in which the children are participating, or where you should vacation together, or who in the family has to be where and at what time—to the extent that our conversations are limited to this level of communication, then the intimacy we experience with our wives will also be limited. What most of us do not realize is that the closeness and connection that we want with our wives will not be facilitated by the type of communication with which we are most accustomed, report-talk. But rather, the type of intimacy most of us really do desire with our wives is actually a byproduct of one of their dominant communication patterns, rapport-talk.

Level 1: Superficial Conversation

For the past 30 years in class, I have attempted to explain that there are essentially four levels of communication, and each of these levels is important in its own way in establishing and promoting relationships. It isn't as if some levels can be

༚

A happy marriage is a long conversation that always seems too short.

-Andre Maurois

ignored as irrelevant while others become the incessant focus of our communication efforts. But at the same time, if we really do want a developing closeness with the woman we love, then we need to engage in those deeper levels of communication that will actually make this desired intimacy an ongoing reality.

The first level of communication is clearly not a very deep part of the communication process. It largely consists of small talk—the "Have a good day," the "How's your day goin'?" the "How ya doin'?" Such small talk is admittedly superficial, but it is at the same time a very important part of the communication process. It is through such "chit chat" that we recognize the presence of others in our lives and we create a conversational environment that is comfortable and inviting. But this having been said, it must be quickly added that if our conversations consistently fail to go beyond this first level, then we will have a very limited experience of close relationships in our lives.

Level 2: People, Places, And Things

When we proceed to Level 2 conversation, we go beyond the realm of mere small talk, and we begin to impart pieces of information to another person. This is the People / Places / Things level of conversation. We are communicating at this level when what we have to say centers primarily on *people* that we know or *places* that we've been or *someone with whom* we've talked or *something* we've noticed or *projects* we are working on or *factual information* we've learned or *something* we're planning to do or *vacation spots* we'd like to visit or *something* that was said by an acquaintance (and the list goes on).

This People / Places / Things level of communication largely consists of report-talk—that type of communication with which most of us men have the largest amount of experience and the greatest amount of

> ớ
> *Motto for the bride and groom:*
> *We are a work in progress*
> *with a lifetime contract.*
>
> -Phyllis Koss

John Buri

comfort. When we men get together, we can talk for quite a while about the work we do and the activities we are looking forward to and the projects we have going and the sporting events we enjoy. Clearly this is a valuable part of communication with someone we love—the activities we enjoy and the things we spend much of our time doing are important aspects of who we are. When we talk with someone about these sorts of things, we are allowing that person to get to know something about us.

But *what we do* is not a very full picture of *who we are*, and when such report-talk is consistently the deepest level of conversation we experience with the woman we love, then it stands to reason that she would desire more from her times of communication with us. And the truth is, we men desire more from these times of communication as well. Numerous research studies have revealed that when we are asked to explain the type of intimacy we desire with the woman we love, the explanations provided don't differ from those of our wives. When we are asked to describe the type of communication that we desire in order to engender greater closeness with the woman we love, these descriptions actually mirror those of our wives.[9]

> ❦
> *This communicating of a man's self to his friend works two contrary effects: for it redoubleth joys and cutteth griefs in half.*
>
> -Sir Francis Bacon

A Skills Deficit, Not A Desire Deficit

The truth is, most men desire the very things from communication that our wives do. But for most of us, we have not been afforded the growing-up experiences that make this type of communication an easy thing to come by. As one newly-married man put it: "As soon as my wife and I begin to 'talk intimately,' I feel as if I'm in a whole new territory, as if I've been dropped in the

> ❦
> *Communication is a skill that you can learn. It's like riding a bicycle or typing. If you're willing to work at it, you can rapidly improve the quality of this part of your life.*
>
> -Brian Tracy

Boundary Waters area of Canada without a map, a compass, or a guide. I definitely want to talk more deeply with my wife and to get closer to her through our communication—I love her—but most of the time I feel lost when our conversations go much beyond the projects we are working on and the stuff we have going."

Obviously, most of us carry some communication deficits with us into marriage. It's not that what we desire is blunted, but rather, those skills that would enable us to realize that which we desire—greater intimacy with the woman we love—have not had a prominent place in our growing-up conversational experience.[10] But if each of us looks at our lives, there are lots of skills that we probably didn't develop while growing up—it might be caulking the windows or changing the oil or checking a sump pump or replacing the spark plugs or repairing a leaky faucet

> ❦
>
> *Some people can never hope to become skilled conversationalists until they learn how to put their foot through the television set.*
>
> -M. Dale Baughman

(and lots of others)—and yet many of us have seen the need for these skill sets and therefore have done what is necessary to develop these abilities.

Communication is in many ways no different. It's a skill and like any skill set, it can be learned.[11] Once we see the need for developing better communication skills—and the need is obvious to just about every man who sees his wife as special and wants to nurture a growing closeness with her—then we can learn to communicate at levels beyond the report-talk of Level 2. If we are willing to put forth the effort and we have the patience to persist in the face of flawed attempts—do you remember what it took to replace your first set of spark plugs?—then for most of us, regular communication with our wives at Level 3 and Level 4 can become a reality.[12]

> ❦
>
> *Loneliness is never more cruel than when it is felt in close proximity with someone who has ceased to communicate.*
>
> -Germaine Greer

Level 3: I Wanted To Say More With My Children

When we communicate at Level 3, we begin to reveal what it is that we believe in and what it is we value. Basically at this level of communication, we are letting someone know what's important to us, what motivates us, what makes us tick. My father died when I was twenty-four years old, and I had virtually no idea what was really important to him. I doubt that I am unique in this respect—we just never talked at that level of communication.

Early in my marriage I made a conscious decision that my children would not have a comparable experience with their father. But I realized that before I could ever make this type of communication a reality with my children (especially given the deficit I experienced with my own father), then I was going to have to develop these skills with the closest person in my life, my wife.

> *Don't be the man you think you should be, be the father you wish you'd had.*
>
> -Letty Cottin Pogrebin

The main thing in making Level 3 communication happen is to discuss what it is that you regard as important—basically to reveal what it is that you believe and why you believe it. I have known many couples who have used books of questions/scenarios to facilitate this process.[13] One of my sons and his wife have been using a book titled *If...: Questions for the Soul.* Following are a few of the more than 500 questions raised in this book. "If you could have one thing said about you by someone after your death, what would you want them to say?" "If you could relieve yourself of one burden in life, what would it be?" "If there was one road in life you should not have gone down but did, what would you say it was?" "If you were to recall the most providential moment or experience in your life, what would you say it was?"

Obviously, we can't respond to such questions without letting someone else know what's important to us and what it is that we believe in. For most of us men, such self-revealing communication is a relatively new experience in our lives. And not only is it new—it's also disarming. For most of us, having grown up in a world of status and competition—in other words, having grown up in a world of males—disarming ourselves is an uncomfortable and vulnerable place in which to be. As a result, for many of us men, we avoid going beyond Level 2 communication not only because of a skills deficit, but also because of a long-reinforced urge to hold vulnerability off at arm's length.

> ❦
> *Make sure you have someone in your life from whom you can get reflective feedback.*
>
> -Warren Bennis

Unfortunately, when we do this, we also end up undermining the type of reflectiveness, self-disclosure, and trust that will facilitate the very thing we desire—greater intimacy with the woman we love.

Numerous studies (as well as countless therapy sessions) have revealed that without this type of deeper communication, marital satisfaction and marital stability will be in serious jeopardy.[14] So regardless of whether this type of Level 3 communication flows relatively effortlessly in our marriages or whether we need to prime the communication pump with some of the many canned question books that are available, the important thing is that we do it.

Level 4: Getting Even More Personal

On numerous occasions I have had men ask me what could possibly be deeper than this type of conversation in which we discuss those things that are most important to us and we communicate what it is that we believe in. Admittedly these are very revealing aspects of communication—they say a lot about us beyond what we do. But there is even more that we can reveal to someone whom we love, and it is in the context of marriage (more than any other relationship) that this fourth level of communication is vital.[15]

It is in this Level 4 communication that we begin to share with someone the unique impact that circumstances and events are having on us personally. Recently, when a very promising work-related opportunity was pre-

> ❦
> *A friend is a person with whom I may be sincere. Before him I may think aloud.*
>
> -Ralph Waldo Emerson

sented to me, I knew that my wife, Kathy, would want to know more about my response to this opportunity than simply what I saw as the pros and cons of the situation. She would want to know *where I was at* with the fact that this opportunity had been presented—was I flattered by the offer? Or was I threatened by the challenge? Or was I experiencing undue self-adulation for the recognition? Or was I concerned about the additional work involved? To talk with Kathy about the pros and cons (as I saw them) gave her information about the opportunity (report-talk) and it even revealed some of what I value and what I see as important, but it was not until I talked about the impact of this offer on me personally that Kathy felt as if we had adequately communicated about the topic.

I Had To Learn It The Hard Way

As you may suspect, it was not always the case that I was aware of the need for this level of communication in my marriage. As has too often been the case in my life, I had to learn it the hard way. Even though the research evidence is clear, I had to experience a growing distance from the most important person in my life—nearly to the point of a failed marriage—before I sincerely engaged the task of communication and began to work at revealing to Kathy how I really felt about things that were going on in my life (as well as in our life together).

SENSIBLE EFFORT
BY REASONABLE PEOPLE

- Does your wife know those things that weigh most heavily on your mind?
    - o About your work?
    - o About your friends?
    - o About work around the house?
    - o About your family?
    - o About your marriage?
    - o About yourself?

- Is your wife aware of the most important events in your day?
    - o Before they happen, what they are? Why they are important to you?
    - o After they have happened, how they went? What effect they have had on you?

- Does your wife know those things that have brought you your greatest joys? Your greatest disappointments?
    - o In the last week?
    - o In the last month?
    - o In the last year?

- Is your wife aware of those things that you most hope for? Those things that you most fear?
    - o About your career?
    - o About the many responsibilities you carry?
    - o About your friendships?
    - o About your health?
    - o About your physical attractiveness?
    - o About your family?
    - o About your life with her?

And it is this type of communication that most of our wives long to have in common with us—that we would talk with them about the impact that events and circumstances are having on us personally. And it is this that promotes the type of richness, depth, and closeness with our wives that we had in mind when we first said "I do." Even though most of us have had limited experience with such Level 4 communication, it is a skill that we can develop and it is a skill that will pay huge dividends in our marriages.

The Quiet Whisper

Over the years with my children I have tried to describe this level of communication as that little voice inside of us that quietly whispers when an event happens in our lives. As is typically the case with girls (who have so much more experience with rapport-talk), my daughter quickly and easily mastered the ability to hear "the whispers" within her—whether or not she was willing to honestly reveal what was going on inside of her was another matter, but she clearly had the capacity to do so. My sons, on the other hand, were a different story. Initially the only "voice inside them" that they were in touch with was anger (and often that voice was not whispering). But they, too—through understanding, reflection, and practice—have developed an impressive facility with Level 4 communication.

For example, all of our sons have played some basketball at the collegiate level and when each of them had finished playing the last game of his career, I wanted to spend some time

> *Self-reflection is the school of wisdom.*
> -Baltasar Gracian

talking with him about this reality. I certainly was interested in discussing information about the game and the season—what went well and what could have been done differently—but I was also very interested in what impact this was having on them personally. After nearly 15 years of playing organized ball, it was suddenly over! What were they experiencing? What were they feeling as they faced this stark reality?

When we begin to give someone this type of information about ourselves, then we begin to reveal some deep aspects of who we are. For each of my sons, what they were going through was a little different, but each of them was able to reflect sufficiently to understand what it was that they were feeling—what those quiet whispers were expressing in that place where only they could hear them. And I was honored that they were willing to talk openly with me about those whispers.

In other living creatures the ignorance of themselves is nature, but in men it is a vice.

-Boethius

A Toast

In the process of writing this book, I have had numerous moments of reflection about my own marriage. I have ruminated on the joy of our early love for one another—rich and heartfelt, but largely untested by the adversities inherent in the process of living. I have thought a lot about the many ways in which I was unprepared as a man for my part in making my marriage work. I have lamented again the pain that I caused, and I have been grateful anew that years ago I did not hastily throw away the love of my life. I have recalled again the many ways in which I needed to change so that the things most important to me—my wife, my marriage, my children—might thrive.

And in the end, I am reminded of what I have sometimes told the young men who played basketball for me. What they may have done last month or last week or last night doesn't count for much today. They cannot stand and sulk about yesterday's mistakes nor can they sit back and rest on yesterday's laurels. Each day they have to come and put it all on the line again.

There are no successful marriages. There are only those that are succeeding – or failing.

-Wells Goodrich

And so it is with my marriage. Each day I have to come and put it all on the line again. I have to make it clear *today* that my wife, Kathy, is very special to me, that she is the love of my life, that I value her presence in my life, and that I will again today do what is needed to keep her that way.

When our oldest son married, I gave a toast to him and his beautiful bride. I held up a rich and robust bottle of wine, and I began to pour it into a wine glass. As the glass became full, and the wine began to spill over the sides of the glass, my toast for them (as well as my toast for you) is that your love for one another will be rich and robust and that the wine glass of your marriage will not be able to hold it all—that it will spill over to those around you—your children, your family members, your friends, your neighborhood, your church, your co-workers. This type of love is incredibly life-giving, and we live in a world that is sorely in need of more of it.

> ౪
>
> *They say it takes a village to raise a child, but it takes a lot of strong, stable marriages to create a village.*
>
> -Diane Sollee

ENDNOTES

Introduction: Love Brings Life

1. To learn more about Willard Harley's analogy of the Love Bank, see Harley (2001, 2009).

Chapter #1: It Takes Two

1   The Monitoring the Future Study titled "Family Values: Belief in Marriage and Family Life Remains Strong" (reported by the University of Michigan Institute for Social Research in 2002) revealed that of the more than two thousand young men and women surveyed, 88% of the men and 93% of the women agreed that having a good marriage and family life was extremely important or important to them.

2. Seeing one's partner as special (i.e., having positively biased evaluations of them) has been found to predict: (a) individuals' level of commitment to the relationship (e.g., Gagne & Lydon, 2003; Martz, Verette, Arriaga, Slovik, Cox, & Rusbult, 1998), (b) their willingness to engage in pro-relationship behaviors (e.g., Murray, 1999; Murray & Holmes, 1997; Van Lange, Rusbult, Drigotas, Arriaga, Witcher, & Cox, 1997), and (c) their satisfaction with the relationship to the exclusion of alternative partners (e.g., Johnson & Rusbult, 1989; Murray, Holmes, & Griffin, 1996). This is not meant to imply that one should promote positively biased evaluations of a partner to the exclusion of accurate evaluations (see Neff & Karney, 2005). But nonetheless, as concluded by Gagne and Lydon (2004) in their thorough review of this research literature, while it

is important to have an accurate view of one's partner, it is also very important to maintain positively biased evaluations of them: "Positive bias is important because it sustains felt security; it helps people regulate their relationship feelings through the ups and downs of daily living. Without this bias, it could be difficult to maintain the conviction that the relationship is good and worth pursuing.... Individuals who are accurate but not positively biased are likely to be despondent and resigned to their relationship fate. If the relationship survives, it is likely to be a function of the moral obligation to remain in the relationship..." (p. 335). Stanley (2005) has similarly highlighted a distinction between a marriage commitment that is founded on dedication and one that is founded on constraint: "*Dedication* implies an internal state of devotion to a person or project. It conveys the sense of a forward-moving motivating force, one based on thoughtful decisions you have made to give your best effort. *Constraint* entails a sense of obligation. It refers to factors that would be costs if the present course were abandoned. Whereas dedication is a force drawing you forward, constraint is a force pushing you from behind.... Research has shown that couples who maintain and act on dedication are more connected, happier, and more open with each other. That's because dedicated partners show their commitment in the following very specific ways...: they think more like a team, with a strong orientation toward 'us' and 'we,' they make their partner and marriage a high priority, they protect their relationship from attraction to others, they sacrifice for one another without resentment, (and) they invest themselves in building a future together..." (pp. 23-24).

3.   Wood (2012) summarized the evidence supporting the importance of non-verbal communication in this way: "Scholars estimate that nonverbal behaviors account for 65% to 93% of the total meaning of communication (Birdwhistell, 1970; Mehrabian, 1981)" (p. 129). In other words, at most, 35% of the meaning derived in two-person communication is based upon the verbal content of the message that is spoken; over 65% of the meaning is extracted from the many non-verbal components of the communication, for example,

eye contact, gestures, tone of voice, inflections, facial expressions, pauses, and body movements.

4. The experience of the marital bond between husbands and wives as well as the various factors that contribute to this bond have been investigated by numerous researchers (e.g., Clements, Cordova, Markman, & Laurenceau, 1997; Gottman & DeClaire, 2002; Gottman & Silver, 2012; Goulston & Goldberg, 2002; Reid, Dalton, Laderoute, Doell, & Nguyen, 2006; Seider, Hirschberger, Nelson, & Levenson, 2009; Stanley, 2005), and the conclusion from this research has been clear and consistent: those couples who develop a bond in their marriage (a sense of team or "we-ness") tend to experience the greatest levels of marital stability and satisfaction.

5. Periodically in this book there will be references made to some of the differences between men and women in areas such as relationship motivation, intimacy, communication, and marriage maintenance. A way to think about many of these gender differences is that they are not universally true of men and women in this culture (see Hyde, 2005), but rather, as suggested by Fletcher (2002), they may apply to as much as 70% of the population.

6. Anthropologists Maltz and Borker (1982) have summarized research describing differences in the communication patterns of boys and girls when participating in their favorite play activities. One of these differences highlighted by Tannen (2007) is that boys' games are much more apt to have "elaborate systems of rules" that will frequently be used to regulate play behavior and to mitigate conflicts.

7. Ninety-two percent of Americans surveyed for the Roper Center Data Review (1998) responded that a very important goal in their lives is to have a successful marriage. A more recent survey by the Pew Research Center (Cohn, 2013) reported that eighty-four percent of Americans still see a successful marriage as a very important life goal.

8. Numerous researchers have reported that declines in marital closeness and satisfaction over the first few years of marriage are typical (e.g., Bradbury & Karney, 2004; Creasey & Jarvis, 2009; Huston, McHale, & Crouter, 1986;

Kurdek, 1999; Scott, Rhoades, Stanley, Allen, & Markman, 2013;Smith, Vivian, & O'Leary, 1990).

9. This summary statement of the customary declines in marital satisfaction was offered by Vangelistic and Huston (1994).

10. Research has revealed that for some individuals, an appearance of optimism is little more than a "positive illusion" (Robins & Beer, 2001). Such individuals tend to optimistically believe that they will experience success in virtually all of their endeavors, but they are quick to give up easily or to retreat into wishful thinking when the task becomes more difficult than was initially anticipated (Aspinwall & Brunhart, 1996; Chang, 1998). In contrast, individuals who manifest a "realistic optimism" tend to be direct problem solvers, actively engaging the task at hand and persisting in the face of difficulty (Schneider, 2001).

11. In reviewing the literature concerning divorce and remarriage, Cox (2006) stated: "Most studies comparing the divorce rates of first marriages with those of second marriages report that a remarriage is more likely to break up than a first marriage" (p. 505).

12. Wegscheider-Cruse (1989) offered the following (edited) explanation of enabling: "Even at a relatively early stage, the people's behaviors are already becoming so unhealthy and irresponsible that the natural consequences of those behaviors threaten to overwhelm them—if they should have to face them. But they rarely do. The people around them, especially those who love them or whose well-being is bound up with theirs, step in and protect them from those consequences. As the problem behaviors progress, enablers step in more often and with more elaborate protection. The effect is to deflect the hand of fate and soften its blow.... They pinch-hit for them, hide their mistakes, alibi or lie for them (even to themselves)... An enabling person often acts out of a sincere, if misguided, sense of love and loyalty... Most enablers I have known do not even see their actions as choices; they honestly feel they have no alternatives. 'If I didn't take over, who would?'" (pp. 89-90). For those readers who would like to better understand the dynamics

behind enabling behavior (and what to do to change it), please see: *The Intimacy Factor* (by Pia Mellody and Lawrence Freundlick), *How to Break Your Addiction to a Person* (by Howard Halpern), *Addicted to Love* (by Stephen Arterburn, and *Is it Love or Is it Addiction?* (by Brenda Schaeffer).

13. For most people, becoming more informed is the first step in overcoming problem behaviors. An excellent resource for recommended books and internet resources has been provided by Norcross, Santrock, Campbell, Smith, Sommer, and Zuckerman (2003).

14. Using an Oral History Interview, Buehlman, Gottman, and Katz (1992) found that the fondness with which couples remembered their early years of dating and marriage was strongly predictive of marital stability with nearly 94% accuracy. In commenting on this research, Kantrowitz and Wingert (2002) stated: "Gottman says one quick way to test whether a couple still has a chance is to ask what initially attracted them to each other. If they recall those magic times (and smile when they talk about them), all is not lost. 'We can still fan the embers'" (p. 87).

15. Waite and Gallagher (2000) offered this summary statement of Linda J. Waite's tabulations from wave 1 (in 1987-1988) and wave 2 (in 1992-1994) of the National Survey of Families and Households.

16. Amato and Booth (1997) offered this conclusion based upon their extensive study of divorce and remarriage.

17. In *The Case for Marriage,* Waite and Gallagher (2000) have presented a seminal review of over 150 empirical investigations of marriage. This review has clearly elucidated the numerous benefits afforded married couples. More recently, Parker-Pope (2010) has summarized numerous research studies indicating the benefits of married life.

18. Reviews of cognitive psychology (e.g., Eysenck, 2012; Smilek, Sinnett, & Kingstone, A. (2013) have reported on the importance of selective attention in our processing of information.

19. For a detailed description of studies investigating the effects of gratitude, see Robert Emmons' (2007) book titled *Thanks! How the New Science of Gratitude Can Make You Happier.*

20. Cancian and Gordon (1988) reviewed articles in popular women's magazines since 1900 and reported that responsibility for the success of heterosexual romantic relationships is more frequently given to women than it is to men. Ragsdale (1996) investigated the actual behaviors of men and women in 103 marriages and he reported results consistent with these purported expectations. Similarly, Heaton and Blake (1999) confirmed these findings with a sample of 4,587 married couples. They reported that compared to their husbands, (a) wives were more sensitive to relationship problems in the marriage and (b) wives were inclined to take greater responsibility for relationship maintenance in the marriage.

21. In his book entitled *Knight: My* Story, Bobby Knight (formerly of Indiana University and currently at Texas Tech University) stated: "We talk in coaching about 'winners'— kids, and I've had a lot of them, who just will not allow their team to lose. Coaches call that a will to win. I don't. I think that puts the emphasis in the wrong place. Everybody has a will to win. What's far more important is having the will to *prepare* to win" (p. 20).

Chapter #2: Loving The Love Of Your Life

1. This clear summary of the benefits of married life was offered by Waite and Gallagher (2000, p. 174).

2. Burgess and Locke (1945) wrote a sociology textbook entitled *The Family: From Institution to Companionship*, and in this text they described the family shift that was occurring in this country from what they termed an "institutional" form of marriage to a "companionship" model of marriage. In the words of Burgess and Locke (from the first chapter of this text): "The basic thesis of this book is that the family has been in historical times in transition from an institution with family behavior controlled by the mores,

public opinion, and law to a companionship with family behavior arising from the mutual affection and consensus of its members. The companionship form of the family is not to be conceived as having already been realized but as emerging.... The most extreme theoretical formulation of the institutional family would be one in which its unity would be determined entirely by the social pressure impinging on family members. The ideal construction of the family as a companionship would focus upon the unity which develops out of mutual affection and intimate association of husband and wife and parents and children" (p. 27). It is interesting to note that by the time the third edition of this text had been published (Burgess, Locke, & Thomes, 1963), only six pages were given to the description and explanation of the institutional family, and most of these references were to a passing model of family life, for example: "With the decline in its institutional functions, the stability of the family comes more and more to depend on the affection and congeniality of its members and less and less on their conceptions of duty and convention. The family becomes less an institution andmore a companionship" (p. 73). And by the time the fourth edition of this book had been published (Burgess, Locke, & Thomes, 1971), the index was void of any references to the institutional family. Authors of current marriage and family textbooks consistently point out that most Americans marry for love; for example, Cox (2002) stated: "The ultimate in human relationships for most Americans is the steady, time-honored, and sought-after combination of love and marriage. When Americans are asked, 'Why do you want to marry?' they often reply, 'Because I love [this person]. So we Americans marry for love" (p. 58)

3. Numerous authors have discussed the positive benefits of expressions of affection for marital satisfaction (e.g., Gottman, 1994c; Gottman & Silver, 1999; Huston & Geis, 1993; Huston & Houts, 1998; Patz, 2002; Scott, Rhoades, Stanley, Allen, & Markman, 2013; Waldinger, Schulz, Hauser, Allen, & Crowell, 2004). As one might suspect, a decline in the overt displays of affection has been

implicated in the process of couples loving one another less (e.g., Bradbury & Karney, 2004; Huston, Caughlin, Houts, Smith, & George, 2001; Huston, Niehuis, & Smith, 2001) and their subsequent inclination toward divorce (e.g., Gigy & Kelly, 1992; Kelly, 1982)

4. Research (e.g., Guldner, 1996; Van Horn, Arnone, Nesbitt, Desilets, Sears, Giffin, & Brudi,1997) has revealed that long-distance romantic relationships are often adversely effected by the geographical separation of the romantic partners. Among the adverse effects reported are reduced self-disclosure, a weakened sense of companionship, increased depressive symptoms, and a decrease in satisfaction with the relationship.

5. Elizabeth Barrett Browning wrote the poem entitled "How Do I Love Thee, Let Me Count the Ways."

6. Extensive research has verified that men have been socialized to emphasize success and personal accomplishments, sometimes to the relative exclusion of relationship concerns. Women, on the other hand, have been raised from their earliest years to give careful attention to relational issues, for example, interpersonal connections, relationship sensitivity, and expressions of affection. Several authors have provided reviews and descriptions of these research findings (e.g., Barnett & Rivers, 1996; Cross, Bacon, & Morris, 2000; Jordan, 1991; Tannen, 2007; Wood, 1996).

7. A couple comments should be made here concerning the periodic discussions in this book of differences between men and women. As was suggested previously, a way to think about these differences is that they may apply to approximately 70% of men and women. In other words, in the present context there are some men (approximately 30%) whose growing up experiences have facilitated a fairly well-developed sensitivity to expressions of affection and relationship maintenance whereas there are some women (approximately 30%) for whom, based upon their socialization, an achievement focus is far more important than is a relational focus. Another point to keep in mind is that whenever gender comparisons are made, a reader should be careful not to therefore end up making a stereotyped

judgment based upon those differences. For example, it is legitimate to conclude that such differences in relationship sensitivity do exist between men and women; however, it is not legitimate to see an acquaintance (e.g., John) and to conclude that simply because he is a male, he is therefore going to be less effective at relationship maintenance than is a woman.

8.   The relationship between work stress and reduced marital satisfaction has repeatedly been documented (e.g., Bolger, DeLongis, Kessler, & Wethington, 1989; Leiter & Durup, 1996; Roberts & Levenson, 2001).

9.   Numerous authors (e.g., Beck, 1995; Burns, 1999; Copeland & McKay, 2002; McKay, Davis, & Fanning, 1981, 2011; Persons, 1989) have discussed the deleterious consequences of treating one's emotions as an accurate reflection of reality and accepting them as an appropriate barometer for how one ought to respond to current circumstances. McKay et al. described the problems with this type of thinking (which has been termed emotional reasoning) in this way: "At the root of this distortion is the belief that what you feel must be true. If you *feel* like a loser, then you must *be* a loser... If you *feel* angry, someone must have taken advantage of you. All the negative things you *feel* about yourself and others must be true because they feel true. The problem with emotional reasoning is that emotions by themselves have no validity" (pp. 22-23). The negative consequences of this type of thinking are further complicated by the conviction that how one feels is outside of their personal control. Such a belief leaves people (and their relationships) at the mercy of whatever their current feeling state happens to be. The truth is that how a person feels at any given point in time is not simply thrust upon us by external circumstances, but rather, we do have some control over how we feel (and with this control comes some level of responsibility). Burns described it this way: "Many people believe that their bad moods result from factors beyond their control... Some people attribute their blue moods to their hormones or body chemistry. Others believe that their sour outlook results from some childhood event that has long been forgotten and buried

deep in their unconscious. Some people argue that it's realistic to feel bad because they're ill or have recently experienced a personal disappointment... These theories are based on the notion that our feelings are beyond our control. If you say, 'I just can't help the way I feel,' you will only make yourself a victim of your misery—and you'll be fooling yourself, because you *can* change the way you feel" (p. 3).

10. Kayser and Himle (2002) discussed key dysfunctional beliefs that serve to undermine the type of connection, closeness, and affection that people actually desire in marriage. One of these is the belief that strong loving thoughts and feelings are needed before overt shows of affection can be expressed. This type of reasoning (typically articulated as: "Once I feel more loving, then I'll start to act that way too") tends to thwart the free flow of overt affection that is so essential to happy marriages.

11. Numerous studies deriving from Festinger's (1957) Cognitive Dissonance Theory (see Cooper & Scher, 1994, for a review) and Bem's (1972) Self-Perception Theory (see Fazio, 1987, for a review) have revealed that an effective way to change how you are thinking and how you are feeling is to change how you are acting. Some of the implications deriving from hundreds of these studies are: if you want to be happier, then smile more and be more pleasant; if you want to be more outgoing, then behave in a more outgoing and talkative manner; if you want to experience greater confidence, then act as if you have that confidence; and if you want to feel more loving, then be more affectionate. In her groundbreaking work on the process of spouses gradually loving one another less ("disaffection"), Kayser (1993) stated: "Often disaffected spouses want to wait until their feelings change before attempting to engage in new behaviors. However, it is important that....the spouses adhere to the 'as if' principle, that is, act *as if* they have the feelings rather than waiting for the feelings to change first" (p. 147).

12. Frank Pittman is a recognized expert marriage therapist, and he issued this statement (Pittman, 1997, p. 311) based upon his many years of experience working with troubled marriages.

13. For excellent reviews of the literature on the importance of religious involvement in the success of marriage, see Mahoney, Pargament, Tarakeshwar, and Swank (2008), Paloutzian and Park (2013), Spilka, Hood, Hunsberger, and Gorsuch (2009), and Welch (2010).

Chapter #3: Talk To Me Like You Love Me

1. Baucom and Epstein (1990) discussed several beliefs held by spouses that serve to undermine marital satisfaction and marital stability. One of these highly destructive beliefs is the idea that "you don't have to be polite to your partner, as you would be to an acquaintance, friend, or stranger" (p.319). In an attempt to describe the frequently rapid demise of courtesy among newly-weds, Gottman (1994c) stated: "One of the first things to go in a marriage is politeness. In some ways this simply reflects increasing comfort. But it leads to taking one another for granted, and it can lead to rudeness. The difference between the conversation of spouses and people who are strangers is that the married couples are far less polite to each other than to the strangers" (pp. 65-66).

2. Numerous studies (e.g., Baucom & Burnett, 1993; Caughlin, Huston, & Houts, 2000; Gottman, 1979; Huston & Vangelisti, 1991; Johnson, Cohan, Davila, Lawrence, Rogge, Karney, Sullivan, & Bradbury, 2005; Noller & Feeney, 1998) have revealed that spouses' negative behaviors toward one another are associated with increased marital conflict, decreased marital satisfaction, increased marital disengagement, increased marital distress, and decreased marital stability. For an excellent review of this literature, see Karney and Bradbury's (1995) meta-analysis of over 115 longitudinal studies (representing over 45,000 marriages) investigating factors related to marital quality and stability.

3. Several studies have revealed that the negativity of husbands frequently has more harmful consequences for the marriage than does the negativity of wives (e.g., Gaelick, Bodenhausen, & Wyer, 1985; Huston & Chorost, 1994; Levenson & Gottman, 1985; Pasch & Bradbury,

1998; Roberts, 2000; Waldinger, Schulz, Hauser, Allen, & Crowell, 2004). One explanation for this relatively robust finding is that women have been socialized to derive a sense of personal well-being and self-worth from the approval they are receiving, especially in family and marital contexts. Therefore, a husband's negativity may signal to his wife a lack of approval and acceptance, and consequently a devaluing of her in his life (e.g., Gaelick, Bodenhausen, & Wyer, 1985; Huston & Chorost, 1994; Krokoff, 1987, 1990). An alternative explanation is that men are simply less sensitive to signs of connection (or lack thereof) in a relationship than are their wives and therefore husbands are less inclined to notice (and to be effected by) negativity in the marriage (e.g., Hawkins, Carrere, & Gottman, 2002; Huston & Vangelisti, 1991; Noller, 1984).

4. Gottman (e.g., Gottman, 1994c; Gottman. Coan, Carrere, & Swanson, 1998; Gottman & Levenson, 1999) has found that a high positive-to-negative ratio of interactions between husbands and wives is strongly predictive of a happy marriage—a ratio of at least five to one is optimal. In the words of Gottman (1994a), if you want a happy and satisfying marriage, "amazingly, we have found that it all comes down to a simple mathematical formula: no matter what style your marriage follows, you must have at least five times as many positive as negative moments together" (p.29).

5. Glenn (1996) found that 93% of Americans say that having a happy, loving marriage is one of their most important personal goals in life. Furthermore, Waite and Gallagher (2000) reported that over "70% of adult Americans believe that 'marriage is a lifelong commitment that should not be ended except under extreme circumstances'" (p. 25).

6. Prochaska, Norcross, and DiClemente (1994) have described the stages people go through as they wrestle to change problem behaviors in their lives. They have made it clear that gaining knowledge about the problem behavior is a key component in successful change efforts. To this end, anyone interested in furthering their understanding of specific types of problem behaviors are referred to Norcross

et al. (2003). These authors have compiled a list of self-help books, internet resources, and relevant movies germane to a variety of behavioral disorders (ranging from Anger and Anxiety Disorders to Weight Management and Women's Issues).

7. Numerous authors (e.g., Baucom & Epstein, 1990; Fitzpatrick, 1988; Gottman & Silver, 1999; Holtzworth-Munroe & Stuart, 1994; Rusbult, Verette, Whitney, Slovik, & Lipkus, 1991) have reported that couples' high relationship-focused standards are predictive of several indices of marital success.

8. This summary statement of the benefits of high marital expectations was offered by Gottman and Silver (1999, p. 262).

9. Several years ago, Kiley (1983) expressed a concern that there were growing numbers of men in this country who struggled with what he termed "The Peter Pan Syndrome"—men whose reticence to take on adult responsibilities prompted them to remain interpersonally unattached for as long as possible. In the words of Peter Pan (in his response to Mrs. Darling): "No one is going to catch me, lady, and make me a man. I want always to be a little boy and to have fun" (Kiley, p. 22). The men described by Kiley variously resisted the entanglements of personal commitments and loving connections. Each in his own way pursued a life course marked by individualism and personal freedom, and even though many of these men married, they still remained independent, self-interested, and interpersonally disconnected. During the ensuing years, this theme has been repeatedly developed (e.g., Biddulph, 2003; Blankenhorn, 1996; Ehrenreich, 1987; Faludi, 2000; Kimmel, 1996; Levant, 1995; Newell, 2004; Pittman, 1993; Popenoe, 1996; Sax, 2007). In these works, there have been various attempts to explain the etiology of this interpersonal detachment by men, its many manifestations (in dating relationships as well as in marriages) have been described, and some of its deleterious consequences have been argued. And running through all these works has been the contention that the struggles of men in this country

to transcend self-interest and to fully engage in the type of connections that love entails are not rare occurrences witnessed only within a clinical setting, but rather, they are more and more becoming the norm.

10. Marriage expert Frank Pittman (1998) summarized the importance of giving yourself to your marriage when he stated that marriage doesn't work "unless you are in it all the way" (p. 192). He went on to explain this by using an analogy of swimming: "Swimming instructors who teach drown-proofing have learned that drowning occurs when people are afraid of the water and struggle to stay above it. If they went ahead and immersed themselves in the water, they would find they could float securely, breathe comfortably, and relax totally.... Marriage is similar.... Many drown rather then surrender themselves to it. They try to protect themselves from it or win at it, and are therefore doomed to failure at such a simple but completely engulfing state" (p. 162).

11. Gottman and DeClaire (2002) reported clear evidence that when a man maintains distance in his marriage, disregarding his wife's "bids for connection" (either "turning against" or "turning away from" these opportunities for closeness with her), then he is much more apt to end up with an unhappy marriage. But when a husband consistently "turns toward" these opportunities for connection with his wife, then he is likely to have a happy marriage. As Gottman and DeClaire put it: "We can conclude from [our research findings] that men may hold a significant key to determining whether or not their marriages will succeed. While wives' attention to their husbands' needs is always important, it's the additional benefit of the husbands' mindfulness that puts the relationship over the top, giving the couple a much better chance of a long, happy marriage" (p. 56). Gottman has offered extensive practical advice to those couples who would like to take greater advantage of their many daily opportunities for connection with one another (see Gottman, 1994c, 1999, 2011; Gottman & DeClair, 2002; Gottman & Silver, 1999).

12. A large body of empirical evidence on relational maintenance has consistently revealed that human relationships thrive on efforts to maintain and enhance existing relational

connections and that they decay as such efforts are minimized (e.g., Baker, McNulty, Overall, Lambert, & Fincham, 2013; Dindia, 2000; Dindia & Canary, 1993; Masuda & Duck, 2002; Ragsdale, 1996; Stafford & Canary, 2006; Vogl-Bauer, 2003; Weigel & Ballard-Reisch, 2008. This proposition was succinctly articulated by Canary and Stafford (1994) when they stated: "All relationships require maintenance behaviors or else they deteriorate" (p. 7). Similarly, Canary, Stafford, and Semic (2002) had this to say about relational maintenance within the marital context: "Spouses need to engage continually in maintenance activities…. The efficacy of most maintenance strategies depends on their continued use" (p. 403).

13. Research has revealed that the demands of employment responsibilities outside the home are taking an increasing toll upon marriage and family life. For a review of relevant empirical literature in this research area, see Johnson (2003) and Perry-Jenkins, Repetti, and Crouter (2000).

14. Lemasters (1957) suggested several years ago that parenthood often presents a particularly difficult period of transition for married couples, negatively impacting marital satisfaction. These early findings have been confirmed repeatedly in subsequent research studies (e.g., Belsky & Kelly, 1994; Cowan & Cowan, 1992; Lower, 2005; Pollmann-Schult, 2014; Twenge, Campbell, & Foster, 2003).

15. Doherty (2013) has made a convincing case that there is much in our American culture that tends to undermine marriage and family life. I would recommend this book for any couple who desires a successful marriage and who feels that they are constantly rowing upstream against the currents of a culture that make it difficult to find the time and energy necessary to create the marriage they desire.

16. Gottman (e.g., Gottman, 1999; Gottman & Silver, 1999) has emphasized the need for couples to be cognizant of early indications of potential problems in their relationship.

17. Glass (2002, 2003) has made it clear that the work environment is increasingly providing a fertile ground for the spawning of marital infidelity. In fact, Mulliken (1998) has stated that "more than 70 percent of affairs start in

the workplace" (p. 18). Any reader interested in gaining a greater understanding of the dynamics surrounding the development of work-related affairs is referred to Glass' (2003) book entitled *NOT "Just Friends."*

Chapter #4: Keeping The Flames Of Love Alive

1. Early research into the contrast effect (e.g., Kenrick & Gutierres, 1980; Melamed & Moss, 1975) employed the repeated exposure of males to pictures and videos of beautiful women. It was found that after such exposure, the judgments by these males of the attractiveness of other women were significantly more negative.

2. More recent studies of this contrast effect have employed pictures of physically attractive women as well as popular erotica, and it has been found that after exposure to such stimuli: (a) men judged their current partners as less satisfying (Kenrick, Neuberg, Zierk, & Krones, 1994; Zillman & Bryant, 1988a), (b) they rated themselves to be less in love with their wives (Kenrick, Gutierres, & Goldberg, 1989), (c) they rated their partners as having less sexual appeal (Bergner & Bridges, 2002; Weaver, Masland, & Zillman, 1984), (d) they reported lower commitment to their partners (Gutierres, Kenrick, & Partch, 1999), and (e) they judged their partners as less attractive and less desirable (Malamuth, 1984; Schneider, 2000; Zillman & Bryant, 1988b).

3. For those interested in further evidence about the deleterious effects of pornography use, please see Fagan (2009), Lambert, Negash, Stillman, Olmstead, & Fincham (2012), Maltz and Maltz (2008), Manning (2006), Owens, Behun, Manning, and Reid (2012), and Struthers (2009).

4. Kupers (1993) offered this apt description of some of the advantages of the pornographic woman (p. 82). A little later he added these comments: "It is frightening how easily men are able to split their time between the social place where a sensitive man tries not to devalue women and the secret place—in one's head as well as in the video booth—where the objectification of women is permissible... But the fact

that a man goes to that secret place, and essentially leaves a part of himself there when he returns to his lover, means their intimacy cannot be complete. For instance, every time his partner asks him what is on his mind while he happens to be thinking about a pornographic image, he feels he must lie to her. The little lies accumulate until his partner begins to complain he is not really present in the relationship. And he is not. Freud enjoyed telling the story of the 'free house,' the point in a town where no arrests would be made, no matter what the crimes of people assembled there. 'How long would it be before all the riff-raff of the town had collected there.' Pornography is like the free house: that secret place becomes the place where all secret thoughts go, and as the secrets accumulate there the quality of a primary relationship deteriorates" (p. 83).

5. McCarthy and McCarthy (2003) stated that the four components of sexual functioning are: (a) desire, (b) arousal, (c) orgasm, and (d) satisfaction. Many people are surprised to discover that "the number one sexual problem facing American couples is inhibited sexual desire" (p. 3).

6. Clark and Hatfield (1989) instructed an attractive confederate to approach strangers of the opposite sex and ask them one of three questions: (a) "Would you go on a date with me?" (b) "Would you come over to my apartment?" or (c) "Would you go to bed with me?" For the female participants in this study, 50% agreed to go on a date, 6% agreed to go to the man's apartment, and none of them agreed to have sex. For the male subjects, 50% agreed to the date, but an even greater percentage of males agreed to go to the woman's apartment (69%) and to go to bed with her (75%). Comparable findings were obtained in two separate studies.

7. These summary statements were presented by Baumeister, Catanese, and Vohs (2001) following their thorough review of the literature concerning gender differences and the strength of the sex drive (pp. 269, 246, 269).

8. Reviews of the research (e.g., Davies, Katz, & Jackson, 1999; Peplau, 2004; Strong, DeVault, & Sayad, 2003) have consistently emphasized the fact that compared to men, the sexual desire of women is much more dependent upon the

intimate, romantic, and committed nature of the relationship. Schnarch (1997) has suggested that for married men and women who work at maturing (both as individuals and as a couple), wives will often become more interested in sexual connection and their husbands will become more interested in emotional connection. It is then that the intimate sexual vitality which most couples have hoped for in their marriage can begin to be realized.

9. Based upon her investigations, Sprecher (2002) has speculated that the relationship satisfaction is more closely linked to sexual satisfaction for men than it is for women.

10. Sometimes people wonder why men typically have a stronger sex drive than do women. Patricia Love (in her book, *The Truth About Love*) succinctly explained it this way: "When I was conducting the research for the book *Hot Monogamy*, I took a healthy dose of testosterone under a doctor's supervision. Let me tell you, it is very different having a strong sex drive! While I was on that drug I thought about sex. I fantasied about sex. I wanted sex. Sexual thoughts came into my mind uninvited. I made sexual innuendoes. I looked at men sexually…without frequent sex, I became irritable. I don't think any research study, any interview, or any book could have convinced this low-testosterone person what it was like to be high in testosterone. It was a real eye-opener, and it humbled me appropriately. Before I had that experience, it was easy for me to be insensitive to my partner's needs, but afterward, I understood what it was like lying on the other side of the bed" (p. 118).

11. Advice columnist Ann Landers addressed the issue of sexual enjoyment among married couples, and the responses she received were described by Cox (2002): "Ann Landers queried her readers on the question: 'Has your sex life gone downhill after marriage? If so, why?' She received over 140,000 replies from the United States as well as other countries. The respondents were nearly evenly divided between men and women. In her words: 'The verdict was clear. Eighty-two percent said sex after marriage was less exciting. The adjectives that turned up most frequently were: boring, dull, monotonous, routine. The message came

equally from men and women'" (p. 245). Admittedly such responses (to a public advice columnist) likely overstate the problem, but Olson and Olson (2000) reported that based upon the responses of 21,501 married couples, a majority of these couples (57%) felt that their sexual relationship was not satisfying and nearly two thirds of these couples (62%) stated that they had to work at maintaining interest in and enjoyment from their marital sex.

12. The sex experts Barry and Emily McCarthy reported that the two most common sexual problems experienced by married couples in this country are (a) inhibited sexual desire and (b) discrepancies in sexual desire (McCarthy & McCarthy, 2003). They make it clear that the way to rekindle sexual desire in a marriage is not by experimenting with sexual techniques or by artificially fanning the flames of sexual passion: "Sex is more than genitals, intercourse, and orgasm. Sexuality involves attitudes, feelings, perceptions, and values... Comfort, attraction, and trust nurture desire" (pp. 7, 9).

Chapter #5: The Crucible Of Conflict

1. A large majority (86%) of the 1,003 young adults sampled by Whitehead and Popenoe (2001) agreed that marriage involves a lot of "hard work."These findings were reported as part of *The State of Our Unions*, an annual report published by The National Marriage Project, which is housed at Rutgers University. The National Marriage project was initiated in response to the growing dearth of information on the state of family life in this country. The inaugural edition (Popenoe & Whitehead, 1999) of *The State of Our Unions* opened with the following statement: "Amid reports of America's improving social health, we hear little about the state of marriage. How is marriage faring in American society today? Is it becoming stronger or weaker? Sicker or healthier? Better or worse? Answers to these questions from official sources have been hard to come by. The federal government issues thousands of reports on nearly every dimension of American life, from what we eat to how many hours we commute each day.

But it provides no annual index or report on the state of marriage. Indeed, the National Center for Health Statistics, the federal agency responsible for collecting marriage and divorce data from the states, recently scaled back this activity. As a consequence, this important data source has deteriorated. The National Marriage Project seeks to fill in this missing feature in our portraits of the nation's social health with *The State of Our Unions*" (p. 3).

2.   Most marriage theorists agree that cconflict in marriage should be expected. As Howell and Jones (2010) put it, "Some couples say that they never fight. While that sounds wonderful, it may be a danger sign, as couples who never have disagreements are more likely to divorce than couples who do... Disagreements between people in a close relationship are inevitable" (p. 88). Eshleman (2003) explained it this way: "Conflict is not viewed as bad or disruptive of social systems and human interactions; instead, conflict is viewed as an assumed and expected part of all systems and interactions.... Because...conflict is quite natural and to be expected, the issue is not how to avoid conflict but how to manage and/or resolve it. In so doing, the conflict, rather than being disruptive or negative, may force change and perhaps make relationships stronger and more meaningful than they were before" (p. 19). Similarly, the importance of healthy conflict resolution was emphasized by Markman, Stanley, and Blumberg (1994) when they stated: "It's not how much you love one another, how good your sex life is, or what problems you have with money that best predicts the future quality of marriage... The best predictor of marital success is the way you handle conflicts and disagreements" (p. 6).

3.   Numerous authors have emphasized the fact that people's thoughts about their spouse and/or about their marriage strongly shape the quality of their relationship (e.g., Bradbury & Fincham, 1990, 1992; Dattilio, 2010; DeGenova, 2008; Finkel, Slotter, Luchies, Walton, & Gross, 2013; Karney & Bradbury, 2000; McNulty & Karney, 2001; Vangelisti, Corbin, Lucchetti, & Sprague, 1999). It has consistently been reported that those couples who respond to distress

in their marriage with negative attributions about their partner and/or about their relationship tend to experience: (a) more negative emotional responses to their spouse, (b) more frequent negative behaviors toward their spouse, and (c) less satisfaction in their marriage.

4. Benokraitis (2011) reported on the pioneering research suggesting that there are five types of marriages in the U.S.: (a) Conflict-Habituated, (b) Devitalized, (c) Passive-Congenial, (d) Vital, and (e) Total. Approximately fifteen percent of U.S. marriages are Conflict-Habituated.

5. As described by Infante and Rancer (1982), those individuals high in argumentativeness enjoy a good argument; they appreciate the experience of a hardy debate, one in which the pros and cons of an issue are heatedly discussed. Janda (1996) has asserted that such high argumentativeness can have negative consequences for interpersonal relationships, an assertion that has been supported by research revealing that: (a) high argumentative individuals tend to be more close-minded when discussing topics in areas of strong personal preference (Frantz & Seburn, 2003), (b) high argumentativeness is more common among those individuals who have been found to be bullies (Ireland, 2002), and (c) high argumentative people tend to be preferred when seeking a companion in conflict-related situations, but not in social-emotional contexts (Waggenspack & Hensley, 1989).

6. As early as 1938, research revealed that married men were inclined to avoid conflict with their wives (Terman, Buttenweiser, Ferguson, Johnson, & Wilson, 1938). This finding has since been repeatedly confirmed by numerous researchers. Following is a partial listing of the voluminous empirical support for the fact that men tend to avoid conflict in their marriages: Christensen (1987), Eldridge and Baucom (2012), Eldridge, Sevier, Jones, Atkins, and Christensen (2012) Gottman (1993, 1994b, 1994c), Gottman and Silver (1999), Heavey, Layne, and Christensen (1993), Margolin & Wampold (1981), Notarius and Johnson (1982), and Vogel and Karney (2002). Holley, Haase, and Levenson (2013) offered the following summary statement: "Demand-

withdraw is common during relationship conflicts and has been described as one of the central, most retractable, and destructive patterns of marital interaction" (pp. 822-823).

7. Christensen (1988) has been credited with first assigning this term (i.e., "the Demand-Withdraw Pattern") to the common mode of marital interaction in which wives frequently initiate issues for discussion and their husbands consistently avoid such discussions. Numerous researchers (e.g., Ball, Cowan, & Cowan, 1995; Christensen & Shenk, 1991; Christensen & Heavey, 1990; Gottman & Carrere, 1994; Heavey, Christensen, & Malamuth, 1995; Sagrestano, Christensen, & Heavey, 1998) have since confirmed and expanded upon Christensen's initial clarification of this problematic marital pattern of interaction.

8. Some studies have revealed that wives may withdraw from conflict with their husbands (e.g., Heavey, Layne, & Christensen, 1993; Klinetob & Smith, 1996; Sagrestana, Christensen & Heavey, 1998). This withdrawal on the part of wives has consistently occurred in those situations where husbands have initiated discussions of issues in which wives' behavioral changes are expected. Far more typical, however, are instances in which wives initiate such discussions and the husbands withdraw. Summarizing this research, Gottman and Silver (1999) stated: "More than 80 percent of the time it's the wife who brings up sticky marital issues, while the husband tries to avoid discussing them. This isn't a symptom of a troubled marriage—it's true in most happy marriages as well" (p. 115).

9. It has been suggested by Notarius and his colleagues (e.g., Gottman & Notarius, 2000; Notarius, Benson, Vanzetti, Sloane, & Hornyak, 1989; Notarius & Pelligrini, 1987) that the increased demandingness of wives may be a fairly natural response to a perceived experience of not being heard by their husbands. Unfortunately, however, as this demandingness increases, the withdrawal response of men often predictably increases. This cycle of demanding and withdrawing (by wives and husbands, respectively) may then result in a forceful initiation of discussions by wives—

the harsh start-up (see Carrere & Gottman, 1999; Gottman & Silver, 1999; Gottman, Coan, Carrere, & Swanson, 1998).

10. It has frequently been asserted that women have a much stronger relational focus than do men (for literature reviews, see Cross & Morris, 2003; Johnson, 1996; Rugel, 1997; Tannen, 2007; Wood & Fixmer-Oraiz, 2014). As a result of this relational focus, women will often have a much greater sensitivity to relationship issues (for example, cooperation, interest in the concerns of others, ongoing expressiveness, intimacy, active listening) than will men. Consistent with this enhanced relational focus of women, several authors (e.g., Christensen, 1987; Jacobson, 1989; Sagrestano, Heavey, & Chritensen, 1998) have reported that wives typically desire greater closeness in their marriages than do their husbands. This desire for increased closeness in the marriage has been a frequent source of the demandingness of wives.

11. Markman, Stanley, and Blumberg (1994) described husbands' typical responses to conflict with their wives in this way: "*Withdrawal* and *avoidance* are different manifestations of a pattern in which one partner [and as the research has confirmed, this person is usually the husband] shows an unwillingness to get into or stay with important discussions. *Withdrawal* can be as obvious as getting up and leaving the room or as subtle as 'turning off' or 'shutting down' during an argument. The withdrawer may tend to get quiet during an argument or may quickly agree to some suggestion just to end the conversation with no real intention of following through. *Avoidance* reflects the same reluctance to participate in certain discussions, with more emphasis on preventing the conversation from happening in the first place. A person prone to avoidance would prefer it if the difficult topic never came up, and if it did, might manifest the signs of withdrawal described above" (p. 20). Numerous authors (e.g., Christensen & Heavey, 1990; Gottman & Silver, 1999; Gottman, Notarius, Gonso, & Markman, 1976; Heavey, Christensen, & Malamuth, 1995; Markman & Kraft, 1989; Markman, Stanley, & Blumberg, 2010; Stanley, Markman, & Whitton, 2002) have described the deleterious

consequences of such withdrawal (and avoidance) by husbands—for example, decreases in marital satisfaction, poorer relationship functioning, unhealthy conflict resolution behaviors, reduced trust, and poorer communication patterns. As summarized by Baucom, Notarius, Burnett, and Haefner (1990): "As husbands withdraw further from the relationship, their wives are likely to see this withdrawal as yet another problem with the relationship. Husbands' withdrawal is perhaps an even greater issue than the more specific disagreements that were the source of the initial discord" (p. 156). Similarly, Markman (1991) stated: "In our longitudinal studies, one of the best predictors of future distress and divorce is a high level of male withdrawal from real or perceived conflict" (p. 91).

12. As this quote suggests, Gottman (1994c, pp. 159, 160) is convinced that one of the most important pieces of advice he can offer to men who want a successful marriage is to not avoid problem discussions with their wives.

13. Although somewhat counter-intuitive, several researchers (e.g., Gottman & Krokoff, 1989; Karney & Bradbury, 1997; Schilling, Baucom, Burnett, Allen, & Ragland, 2003; Smith, Vivian, & O'Leary, 1990) have documented the value of wives bringing up important issues for discussion in their marriage. While avoidance of problem issues by wives tends to decrease marital conflict in the near-term, such avoidance has been shown to have negative consequences for marital satisfaction in the long run. In the process of discussing such findings, Schilling et al. (2003) stated: "Higher negative communication behaviors in wives may represent wives' willingness to grapple with difficult relationship issues. That is, they are willing to assert themselves and address problems. Although these interactions might be unpleasant at the time, they are likely to be part of a communication process that is important and beneficial for couples in the long run" (p. 49). Similarly, Gottman and Krokoff (1989) suggested: "Behaviors that are functional for 'keeping the peace' in the present may leave unresolved critical areas of conflict that might undermine the relationship over time" (p. 47).

14. It has repeatedly been found that husbands' willingness to listen to their wives, to consider their point of view, and to accept their influence is associated with greater marital stability and increased marital satisfaction (e.g., Coan, Gottman, Babcock, & Jacobson, 1997; Gottman, Coan, Carrere, & Swanson, 1998; Gottman & Levenson, 1999; Gottman & Silver, 1999; Gray-Little, Baucom, & Hamby, 1996; Rusbult, Verett, Whitney, Slovik, & Lipkus, 1991).

15. Gottman and Silver (1999, pp. 113, 111) offered this succinct summary statement concerning the repeatedly-observed success of marriages in which husbands are open to the opinions and influence of their wives.

16. It has been verified in a variety of studies (for literature reviews, see Bradbury, Fincham, & Beach, 2000; Gottman & Notarius, 2002) that in the middle of marital conflicts, husbands will often experience greater physiological arousal than will their wives. Furthermore, it often takes men longer than women to physiologically "settle down" after such arousal. This heightened arousal pattern in men has been implicated in the withdrawal response of husbands when conflict in the marriage does emerge. A valuable antidote to this sometimes intense physiological arousal ("feeling flooded") is the use of techniques designed to reduce that arousal—some of these "self-soothing" techniques have been described in Gottman and Silver (1999).

17. For the sake of their relationship, couples are repeatedly encouraged to set aside time to talk. As stated by Markman, Stanley, and Blumberg: "Most couples do not set aside a regular time for dealing with key issues and problems.The importance of doing so has been suggested by so many marriage experts over the years that it's almost a cliché" (p. 111). For a summary of the research surrounding this encouragement, see DeGenova, Stinnett, and Stinnett (2011), Lauer and Lauer (20009), and Olson, DeFrain, and Skogrand (2011).

18. Gottman (1999) defined criticism as "any statement that implies that there is something globally wrong with one's partner, something that is probably a lasting aspect of the partner's character" (pp. 41-42). Elsewhere, Gottman

articulated the valuable distinction between a complaint and criticism: "There is a world of difference between a complaint and a criticism. A complaint only addresses the specific action at which your spouse failed. A criticism is more global—it adds on some negative words about your mate's character or personality. 'I'm really angry that you didn't sweep the kitchen floor last night. We agreed that we'd take turns doing it' is a complaint. 'Why are you so forgetful? I hate having to always sweep the kitchen floor when it's your turn. You just don't care' is a criticism. A complaint focuses on a specific behavior, but criticism ups the ante by throwing in blame and general character assassination" (Gottman & Silver, pp. 27-28). Christensen and Walczynski (1997) offered the following summary statement of the deleterious marital consequences of criticism: "Among the most consistent findings in this area are that distressed partners criticize…each other more often than non-distressed partners" (p. 251).

19. Lamanna Riedmann, and Stewart (2014), Galvin, Bylund, and Brommel (2011), and Schwartz and Scott (2012) have provided reviews of the literature in which the open, honest, and relatively straightforward communication by spouses has been found to provide long-term benefits to the marriage and to the individuals involved.

20. For practical advice on how to develop negotiation and compromising skills in a marriage context, see Knox and Schacht (2012), Alexander (2013), Bernstein and Magee (2003), Markman, Stanley, and Blumberg (2010), McKay, Davis, and Fanning (2008), and Robinson (2012).

21. Two of the early pioneers in marriage and family therapy, Augustus Napier and Carl Whitaker, suggested that the experience of marriage can sometimes be akin to a crucible (see their book titled *The Family Crucible*). In this book, Whitaker and Napier have presented numerous examples of the intense psychological, emotional, and interpersonal "heat" that can be experienced in the midst of the family crucible, and he has provided lucid illustrations of how such heat can prompt a variety of personal weaknesses to emerge into full view within the family milieu. This theme

has been variously developed since Napier's seminal work; for example, see: "Humor in Family Therapy: Laughter in the Crucible" (1994) by Charles Streff, "Families as the Crucible of Competence in a Changing Social Ecology" (1999) by Don Edgar, *The Crucible of Experience* (2000) by Daniel Burston, and "The Therapist in the Crucible" (2001) by David Schnarch. In their review of the Systems Approach to family therapy, Nichols and Schwartz (2003) have noted the consistent emphasis upon understanding an underlying "crucible experience" when addressing issues of marriage and family functioning.

22. Wallerstein and Blakeslee (1995), authors of the book entitled *The Good Marriage: How and Why Love Lasts*, used extensive interviews with couples from enduring marriages to derive the keys to long-lasting and successful marriages. The couples involved in this study came from a wide variety of social, economic, and educational backgrounds. Some of these couples experienced severe difficulties in their marriages (e.g., serious illness, economic struggles, anger, depression, infidelity). Nonetheless, they all reported a lasting love for their spouse and a genuine satisfaction with their marriage. The key most often mentioned by these living examples of marital success revolved around such phrases as: "feeling well cared for," "feeling respected and cherished," knowing "that they were central to their partner's world," and sharing with their partner the reality that "creating the marriage and the family was the major commitment of their adult life" (p. 329). The authors emphasized that central to these phrases and essential to the experience of marital success by these couples was the repeated willingness by the individuals in these marriages to change for the sake of their partner, for the good of the marriage, and for the benefit of their children. DeGenova and Rice (2005) have devoted an entire chapter of their text reviewing several qualities related to this willingness to change and the concomitant marital success experienced by those spouses who choose to embrace such changes.

23. Wallerstein and Blakeslee (1995) emphasized the importance of mutual accountability by husbands and wives

in successful marriages, and they offered this summary statement (pp. 334) of this key finding from their study.

24. Criticism (and its behavioral partner, contempt) have been repeatedly implicated in the demise of marital love (e.g., Clements, Stanley, & Markman, 2004; Gottman, 1994a, 2011; Gottman & Levenson, 2000; Gottman & Silver, 1999; Johnson, 2002; Matthews, Wickrama, & Conger, 1996; McGonagle, Kessler, & Gotlib, 1993; Pasch & Bradbury, 1998). In fact, Notarius and Markman (1993) have reported evidence that one deeply hurtful comment (a "zinger") "will erase twenty acts of kindness" (p. 28).

25. The benefits to married couples of asking for forgiveness as well as granting forgiveness have been well-documented (e.g., Fincham, 2000, 2004; Fincham, Paleari, & Regalia, 2002; Gordon, Baucom, & Snyder, 2000; McCullough, Rachal, Sandage, Worthington, Brown, & Hight, 1998). Fincham, Beach, and Davila (2004) offered the following summary statement: "Paradoxically, those we love are often the ones we are most likely to hurt. It is a rare person who does not, at some point, feel 'hurt,' 'let down,' 'betrayed,' 'disappointed,' or 'wronged' by his or her relationship partner. When interpersonal transgressions occur in marriage they can elicit strong negative feelings and have the potential to disrupt the relationship. Perhaps not surprisingly, spouses report that the capacity to seek and grant forgiveness is one of the most important factors contributing to marital longevity and marital satisfaction" (p. 72).

Chapter #6: The Heart Of Intimacy: Communication

1. Indifference has been discussed as an important factor in relationship termination (e.g., Baxter & Philpot, 1982; Dindia, 1994) and it has been heavily implicated in the process of marital disaffection (e.g., Crosby, 1991; Gigy & Kelly, 1992; Gottman & Levenson, 2002; Kayser, 1993). As Reik (1976) put it: "The most serious enemy of love is not the hostility but the indifference that one feels toward

the other" (p. 97). Similarly, Cox (2011) poignantly stated: "Indifference is the opposite of love" (p. 76).

2. There is a growing interest on the part of marriage and family researchers in the day-to-day "social support" that married couples provide for one another. Numerous studies have revealed that marital satisfaction and marital quality decrease as husbands and wives respond to their spouses' needs for support in a negative manner (e.g., Carels & Baucom, 1999; Cutrona, 1996; Dehle, Larsen, & Landers, 2001; Johnson, Cohan, Davila, Lawrence, Rogge, Karney, Sullivan, & Bradbury, 2005; Saitzyk, Floyd, & Kroll, 1997). Some of these negative responses to solicitations for support have been overtly aversive (e.g., belittlement, disparagement, criticism), while others have been aversive through a lack of responsiveness (e.g., disinterest, dismissiveness, indifference). Bradbury and Karney (2004) have offered the following summary of the research demonstrating the vital importance of social support to successful marriages: "This evidence indicates that a more basic communication deficit—perhaps a difficulty in setting aside one's own interests and concerns in order to attend to those of the partner and the marriage—operates to place couples at risk for marital dysfunction.... Moreover, the negative affect that couples display during problem solving appears to be more costly to the marriage when social support skills are weak versus strong.... Positive engagement seems to envelop the couple like Teflon, so unskilled behavior and negative emotions do not stick to the couple as they negotiate different tasks and situations" (p. 868).

3. In 2003, the Institute for American Values published a book titled *Hardwired to Connect*. Those readers interested in evidence that the need to love is part of our human nature would do well to read this well-documented work. More recently, other authors have developed this idea in popularized books. For example, in a book for young adults *Unhooked*, Laura Sessions Strepp said: "The need to be connected intimately to others is as central to our well-being as food and shelter. If we don't get it right, we're probably not going to get anything else in life right either" (p. 8).

Similarly, Brene Brown *Daring Greatly* stated: "Love and belonging are irreducible needs of all men, women, and children. We're hardwired for connection—it's what gives purpose and meaning to our lives. The absence of love, belonging, and connection always leads to suffering" (pp. 10-11).

4. Numerous authors have emphasized the fact that if you want a stable and satisfying marriage, then you and your spouse should have a desire to change and to grow throughout your years together (e.g., Bloom & Bloom, 2004; Davisson & Davisson, 2010; Fincham, Stanley, & Beach, 2007; Fowers, 2000; Howell & Jones, 2010; Sternberg, 1991; and Wallerstein & Blakeslee, 1995).

5. The importance of interpersonal intimacy to the ongoing experience of love has been firmly asserted by numerous authors. The interested reader could begin with the following list of references: Bagarozzi (2001a), Demaria, Hannah, and Gordon (2002), McCarthy and McCarthy (1992), Olson and Olson (2000), Sternberg (1988), and Williams, Sawyer, and Wahlstrom (2009).

6. It should not come as a surprise that the positive experience of sexuality between married couples has been found to contribute to marital satisfaction (e.g., Greeff & Malherbe, 2001; McCarthy, 2001; Seccombe & Warner, 2004). But possibly the best explanation of the relationship between sexual satisfaction and marital satisfaction has been offered by McCarthy (1999), who suggested that when sex is going well in a marriage, then it constitutes 15-20% of the relationship; however, when there are sexual problems in a marriage, then sex tends to have a much more powerful role in the marriage (constituting as much as 50-75% of marital satisfaction) —sexual problems are inclined to reduce intimacy and vitality in a marriage.

7. Based upon their seminal review of research into patterns of childhood interactions, Maltz and Borker (1982) suggested that the play of children is anything but mere play. They asserted that the games of little girls and little boys are actually an important part of their socialization into the world of talk, teaching them the what, where, when, why, and how

of communication. Maccoby (1988, 1990) has provided summaries of the empirical research results supporting the assertions of Maltz and Borker. Tannen (1990) popularized much of this work in her book entitled: *You Just Don't Understand: Men and Women in Conversation.* As Tannen stated: "…women speak and hear a language of connection and intimacy, while men speak and hear a language of status and independence…. Where, then, do women and men learn different ways of speaking and hearing?…. Boys tend to play outside, in large groups that are hierarchically structured. Their groups have a leader who tells others what to do and how to do it…. Boys' games have winners and losers and elaborate systems of rules…. Finally, boys are frequently heard to boast of their skills and argue about who is best at what. Girls, on the other hand, play in small groups or in pairs…. Within the group, intimacy is key. Differentiation is measured by relative closeness. In their most frequent games, such as jump rope and hopscotch, everyone gets a turn. Many of their activities (such as playing house) do not have winners and losers…. They don't grab center stage—they don't want it—so they don't challenge each other directly. And much of the time, they simply sit together and talk" (pp. 42-44). Similarly, Glass (1992) summarized the research in this way: "Throughout the socialization period, little boys not only play differently but talk about different things than little girls. Early on in life little girls tend to talk about people—'who is mad at whom' and 'who likes whom.' They will usually talk about their friends. Since most little girls tend to play together in two's or small groups, they will usually tell one another 'secrets' in order to bond their friendship together. These 'secrets' are usually about people…. On the other hand, little boys that age will talk about things and 'activities.' Little boys are usually socialized in groups and mostly talk about their activities—what they all are doing, and who is the 'best' at the activity" (p. 73). The terms "rapport-talk" and "report-talk" were coined by Tannen (1990).

8. It is a common assertion by marriage and family authors that the predominant communication styles of women

(rapport-talk) and men (report-talk) are a source of struggle in many marriages—for example, see Cox and Demmitt (2014), DeGenova and Rice (2005), Gray (2012), Olson and DeFrain (2003), and Schwartz and Scott (2012).

9. Are men and women looking for something different when we each say that we desire intimacy with our partner—in other words, do men and women define intimacy differently? Considerable research suggests that the answer is "no." For example, Reis, Senchak, and Solomon (1985) asked men and women to evaluate the degree of intimacy of several videotaped conversations. No significant gender differences were found when comparing these intimacy judgments of men versus those of women. Similarly, in several other studies (e.g., Burleson & Samter, 1985a; Helgeson, Shaver, & Dyer, 1987; Monsour, 1992; Waring, Tillman, Frelick, Russell, & Weisz, 1980), the descriptions and evaluations of what constitutes intimacy offered by men and women were very similar; both men and women focused on such interpersonal characteristics as emotional expressiveness, affective closeness, and the sharing of personal information. Further research has revealed that not only do men and women define intimacy in a very similar manner, but also: (a) when asked to compare this type of expressive communication versus a communication pattern that is more instrumental (e.g., involving problem-solving or providing information), both men and women view intimate communication patterns as a more effective way to communicate, especially in times of distress (e.g., Burleson & Samter, 1985b; Jones & Burleson, 1997; 2003); (b) both men and women have similar intimacy expectations in their romantic relationships (e.g., Burleson, Kunkel, Samter, & Werking, 1996; Vangelisti & Daly, 1999); and (c) men and women equally value this type of intimacy in their romantic relationships (e.g., Burleson et al., 1996; Kunkel & Burleson, 1999; Sprecher, Metts, Burleson, Hatfield, & Thompson, 1995). For more extensive reviews of this research area, see Kunkel and Burleson (1998) and Reis (1998).

10. Some authors (e.g., Bate & Bowker, 1997; Noller, 1993; Wood, 1997) have asserted that men and women inhabit two distinct cultures, each one having its own expectations for relationship intimacy, its own standards for the sharing of personal information, and its own customs for emotional responsiveness. Furthermore, it is typically suggested by such authors that each set of communication imperatives are equally valid in the development of intimate relationships. The oft-repeated emphasis deriving from this "different cultures" perspective was poignantly summarized by Kunkel and Burleson (1998) when they cited articles addressing the following questions: "Men and women: Can we get along? Should we even try?" More recently, however, this different cultures point of view has received considerable criticism (e.g., Kyratzis, 2001; MacGeorge, Graves, Feng, Gillihan, & Burleson, 2004; Vangelisti, 1997). In summarizing numerous empirical studies, Reis (1998) suggested that men and women do not appear to come from different planets, but rather: "The evidence... indicates that men and women define intimacy and closeness in largely the same way and aspire to essentially the same relationship qualities" (p. 226). The fact of the matter still remains, however, that even though men and women have a similar understanding of what constitutes a good friend and they both similarly desire such friendships in their intimate relationships, we sometimes differ in our capacity to foster those relationship qualities in our marriages. But the research evidence suggests that this fact results less from different notions by men and women of what constitutes intimacy or different understandings of what will promote friendship; rather, these differences more often emerge from the relatively restricted skill sets of men when it comes to sensitive supportive communication. The importance of the development by men of those skill sets that will facilitate close friendships with their wives has been highlighted by Gottman and Silver (1999), who have offered the following conclusion concerning friendship and marital satisfaction: "The determining factor in whether wives feel satisfied with the sex, romance, and passion in their marriage is,

by 70 percent, the quality of the couple's friendship. For men, the determining factor is, by 70 percent, the quality of the couple's friendship" (p. 17). As Gottman and Silver concluded: "So men and women come from the same planet after all" (p. 17).

11. The idea that communication is a skill that can be practiced and refined may be quickly evidenced in the titles of several popular communication books: *Couple Skills: Making Your Relationship Work* (McKay, Fanning, & Paleg, 1994); *Gifts From the Heart: Ten Communication Skills for Developing More Loving Relationships* (Fujishin, 1998); *Communicating Effectively for Dummies* (Brounstein, 2001); *Messages: Building Interpersonal Skills* (Devito, 2004); *Messages: The Communication Skills Book* (McKay, Davis, & Fanning, 1995). In each of these books, the same communication skills are taught to both women and men, and communication experts have made it clear that both women and men are equally capable of mastering these skills.

12. There are not any men who are (simply by virtue of being men) incapable of the communication skills necessary for the development of intimacy. However, this is not meant to imply that all men—or all women, for that matter—will find these communication skills equally easy to develop. In fact, in some instances individuals may be so personally limited that they are virtually incapable (without counseling) of the deep and caring type of communication that is necessary for an ongoing experience of love. A few such instances will be briefly discussed here. This discussion is not meant to provide an exhaustive list of such instances, but rather, it is meant to give the reader a cursory understanding of some warning signs that may signal that an individual's struggles with communication may be rooted in deeper issues in that person's life. **Interpersonal Avoidance:** As described by Oltmanns and Emery (2004), individuals who struggle with severe interpersonal avoidance issues generally experience a pervasive pattern of discomfort in social situations, they tend to have an intense fear of negative evaluation by others, and while they often have a strong desire to be liked by others, their timidity and fear of criticism generally

inhibit them from developing the very relationships they desire. Similarly in the attachment literature, several authors have asserted that intimacy and emotional closeness are the very things that "avoidantly attached" individuals are trying to avoid (e.g., Edelstein & Shaver, 2004; Mashek & Sherman, 2004; Shaver & Hazan, 1993; Tidwell, Reis, & Shaver, 1996). **Narcissism:** Narcissism is characterized by an exaggerated sense of self-importance and a hypersensitivity to the potential criticisms of others. Furthermore, the narcissist's heightened sense of personal special-ness often prevents him or her from empathizing with the feelings and needs of others (Campbell, 2005; Golomb, 1992; Payson, 2002). As stated by Piorkowski (1994): "The grandiosity of narcissists…does not allow us ready access into their intimate zone. They keep intimate partners at a distance…. Their difficulties in being attentive, empathic, and genuinely interested in their intimate partner leave the partner feeling unloved and lonely" (pp. 227-228). With regard to the intimacy struggles of narcissists, Halpern (1990) succinctly stated: "It is difficult if not impossible for narcissists (depending upon the degree of narcissism) to have close, intimate relationships with other people" (pp. 131- 132). **Anger:** The prevalence and destructiveness of persistent problematic anger has been well-documented (e.g., Deffenbacher, 1992; Hightower, 2002; Tavris, 1989; Williams & Williams, 1993). Recurring anger can be especially destructive in personal relationships. Repeated episodes of hostile irritation, indignant fault-finding, and angry tirades will undermine those communication patterns upon which close loving relationships are based. McKay, Rogers, and McKay (1989) described the destructive impact of anger upon intimacy in this way: "Typical defenses against anger include numbness, judging, irritability, attack, withdrawal, revenge, and extreme restriction of response. Once laid down, the barriers make you rigid, and trigger-happy. It's hard to switch from defense to appreciation, from vigilance to any kind of trust. You'll tend to stay in the bunker, rather than risk openness" (p. 35).

13. Following are listed a few of the many books that are available to facilitate deeper levels of communication: *If Questions for the Soul* (McFarlane & Saywell, 1998); *The Hard Questions: 100 Essential Questions to Ask Before You Say "I Do"* (Piver, 2000); *The Book of Questions* (Stock, 1987); *Intellectual Foreplay* (Hogan & Hogan, 2000); *The Marital Compatibility Test: Hundreds of Questions for Couples to Answer Together* (Adams, 2000); and *The Conversation Piece* (Nicholaus & Lowrie, 2000).

14. When happy couples are contrasted with unhappy couples, one of the primary differences that has been found repeatedly is in the area of communication—unhappy couples do not communicate as often or as effectively as happy couples. For extensive reviews of this literature, see Lauer and Lauer (2009), Olson and Olson (2000), Strong and Cohen (2013),and Williams, Sawyer, and Wahlstrom (2009).

15. The day-to-day conversations of couples (both the small discussions and the larger exchanges) are an important part of any successful marriage. Such ongoing patterns of communication facilitate the development of a shared reality, a shared life together, for the couple. As Duck (1994) put it: "Relationships, like conferences, keep going because they are filled with juicy meaning for the partners. *Period.* This juicy meaning is created in talk and the mere occurrence of talk in everyday relationships not only satisfies the partners that the relationship exists and is important *irrespective of the content of the talk*, it also reifies, sustains, and produces the relationship" (p. 51). The importance of everyday conversation to relationship satisfaction has been verified by numerous authors (e.g., Canary & Dainton, 2003; Weigel & Ballard-Reisch, 1999; Wood, 1995). This having been said, however, the emphasis here is on the fact that it is through deeper levels of personal communication that increased couple intimacy can be fostered. Numerous authors have discussed the fact that as self-disclosure increases, couples' interpersonal closeness also increases (e.g., Bagarozzi, 2001b; Benokraitis, 2005; Cox, 2006; Laurenceau, Barrett, & Peitromonaco, 1998; Prager & Roberts, 2004; Reis & Patrick, 1996).

REFERENCES

Adams, S. (2000). *The marital compatibility test: Hundreds of questions for couples to answer together.* Omaha, NE: Addicus Books.

Alexander, S. M. (2013). *Deciding in unity: A practical process for married couples to agree on practically everything.* Chattanooga, TN: Marriage Transformation Press.

Amato, P. R., & Booth, A. (1997). *A generation at risk: Growing up in an era of family upheaval.* Cambridge, MA: Harvard University Press.

Arterburn, S. (2003). *Addicted to "love": Understanding dependencies of the heart: Romance, relationships, and sex.* NY: Vine Books.

Aspinwall, L. G., & Brunhart, S. M. (1996). Distinguishing optimism from denial. *Personality and Social Psychology Bulletin, 22,* 993-1003.

Bagarozzi, D. A. (2001a). *Enhancing intimacy in marriage: A clinician's guide.* NY: Brunner- Routledge.

Bagarozzi, D. A. (2001b). *Enhancing intimacy in marriage: A clinician's handbook.* Atlanta, GA: Taylor and Francis Publishers.

Baker, L. L., McNulty, J. K., & Overall, N. C. (2013). How do relationship maintenance behaviors affect individual well-being? *Social Psychological and Personality Science, 4,* 282-289.

Ball, F. L. J., Cowan, P., & Cowan, C. P. (1995). Who's got the power? Gender differences in partner's perception of influence during marital problem-solving discussions. *Family Process, 34,* 303-321.

Barnett, R. C., & Rivers, C. (1996). *She works / he works.* San Francisco, CA: Harper Collins.

Bate, B., & Bowker, J. (1997). *Communication and the sexes* (2nd ed.). Prospect Heights, IL: Waveland Press.

Baucom, D. H., & Burnett, C. K. (1993). Conflict in marriage: A cognitive / behavioral formulation. In S. Worchel & J. A. Simpson (Eds.), *Conflict between people and groups* (pp. 7-29). Chicago, IL: Nelson-Hall Publishers.

Baucom, D. H., & Epstein, N. (1990). *Cognitive-behavioral marital therapy.* NY: Brunner/ Mazel.

Baumeister, R. F., Catanese, K. R., & Vohs, K. D. (2001). Is there a gender difference in strength of sex drive? Theoretical views, conceptual distinctions, and a review of relevant evidence. *Personality and Social Psychology Review, 5,* 242-273.

Baucom, D. H., Notarius, C. I., Burnett, C. K., & Haefner, P. (1990). Gender differences and sex-role identity in marriage. In F. D. Fincham & T. N. Bradbury (Eds.), *The psychology of marriage: Basic issues and applications* (pp. 150-171). NY: Guilford Press.

Baxter, L. A., & Philpot, J. (1982). Attribution-based strategies for initiating and terminating relationships. *Communication Quarterly, 30,* 217-224.

Beck, J. S. (1995). *Cognitive therapy: Basics and beyond.* NY: Guilford Press.

Belsky, J., & Kelly, J. (1994). *The transition to parenthood: How a first child changes a marriage.* NY: Dell Publishers.

Bem, D. J. (1972). Self-perception theory. In L. Berkowitz (Ed.), *Advances in experimental social psychology* (Vol. 6, pp. 1-62). NY: Academic Press.

Benokraitis, N. V. (2011). *Marriage and families: Changes, choices, and constraints.* Upper Saddle River, NJ: Prentice Hall.

Bergner, R. M., & Bridges, A. J. (2002). The significance of heavy pornography involvement for romantic partners: Research and clinical implications. *Journal of Sex and Marital Therapy, 28,* 193-206.

Biddulph, S. (2003). *The secret life of men.* NY: Marlowe and Company.

Birdwhistell, R. L. (1970). *Kinesics and context: Essays on body motion communication.* Philadelphia, PA: University of Pennsylvania Press.

Blankenhorn, D. (1996). *Fatherless America: Confronting our most urgent social problem.* NY: Harper Collins.

Bloom, L., & Bloom, C. (2004). *101 things I wish I knew when I got married.* Novato, CA: New World Library.

Bolger, N., DeLongis, A., Kessler, R. C., & Wethington, E. (1989). The contagion of stress across multiple roles. *Journal of Marriage and the Family, 51,* 175-183.

Bradbury, T. N., & Fincham, F. D. (1990). Attributions in marriage: Review and critique. *Psychological Bulletin, 107,* 3-33.

Bradbury, T. N., & Fincham, F. D. (1992). Attributions and behaviors in marital interaction. *Journal of Personality and Social Psychology, 63,* 613-628.

Bradbury, T. N., Fincham, F. D., & Beach, S. R. H. (2000). Research on the nature and determinants of marital satisfaction: A decade in review. *Journal of Marriage and the Family, 62,* 964-980.

Bradbury, T. N., & Karney, B. R. (2004). Understanding and altering the longitudinal course of marriage. *Journal of Marriage and the Family, 66,* 862-879.

Brounstein, M. (2001). *Communicating effectively for dummies.* Hoboken, NJ: Wiley Publishing.

Brown, B. (2012). *Daring greatly.* Los Angeles, CA: Gotham Press.

Buehlman, K. T., Gottman, J. M., & Katz, L. F. (1992). How a couple views their past predicts their future: Predicting divorce from an oral history interview. *Journal of Family Psychology, 5,* 295-318.

Burgess, E. W., & Locke, H. J. (1945). *The family: From institution to companionship.* NY: American Book Company.

Burgess, E. W., Locke, H. J., & Thomes, M. M. (1963). *The family* (3rd ed.). NY: American Book Company.

Burgess, E. W., Locke, H. J., & Thomes, M. M. (1971). *The family* (4th ed.). NY: Van Nostrand Reinhold Company.

Burleson, B. R., Kunkel, A. W., Samter, W., & Werking, K. J. (1996). Men's and women's evaluations of communication skills in personal relationships: When sex differences make a difference – and when they don't. *Journal of Personal Relationships, 13,* 201-224.

Burleson, B. R., & Samter, W. (1985a). Consistencies in theoretical and naïve evaluations of comforting messages. *Communication Monographs, 52,* 103-123.

Burleson, B. R., & Samter, W. (1985b). Individual differences in the perception of comforting messages: An exploratory investigation. *Central States Speech Journal, 36,* 39-50.

Burns, D. D. (1999). *The feeling good handbook.* NY: Plume books.

Burston, D. (2000). *The crucible of experience: R. D. Laing and the crisis of psychotherapy.* Cambridge, MA: Harvard University Press.

Campbell, W. K. (2005). *When you love a man who loves himself.* NY: Sourcebooks.

Canary, D. J., & Dainton, M. (Eds.). (2003). *Maintaining relationships through communication: Relational, contextual, and cultural variations.* Mahwah, NJ: Lawrence Erlbaum.

Canary, D. J., & Stafford, L. (1994). Maintaining relationships through strategic and routine interaction. In D. J. Canary & l. Stafford (Eds.), *Communication and relational maintenance* (pp. 3-22). San Diego, CA: Academic Press.

Canary, D. J., Stafford, L., & Semic, B. A. (2002). A panel study of the associations between maintenance strategies and relational characteristics. *Journal of Marriage and the Family, 64,* 395-406.

Cancian, F. M., & Gordon, S. L. (1988). Changing emotion norms in marriage: Love and anger in U.S. women's magazines since 1900. *Gender and Society, 2,* 308-342.

Carels, R. A., & Baucom, D. H. (1999). Support in marriage: Factors associated with on-line perceptions of support helpfulness. *Journal of Family Psychology, 13,* 131-144.

Carrere, S., & Gottman, J. M. (1999). Predicting divorce among newlyweds from the first three minutes of marital conflict discussion. *Family Process, 38,* 293-301.

Caughlin, J. P., Huston, T. L., & Houts, R. M. (2000). How does personality matter in marriage? An examination of trait anxiety, interpersonal negativity, and marital satisfaction. *Journal of Personality and Social Psychology, 78,* 326-336.

Chang, E. C. (1998). Dispositional optimism and primary and secondary appraisal of a stressor. *Journal of Personality and Social Psychology, 74,* 1109-1120.

Christensen, A. (1987). Detection of conflict patterns in couples. In K. Hahlweg & M. J. Goldstein (Eds.), *Understanding major mental disorders: The contribution of family interaction research* (pp. 250-265). NY: Family Process Press.

Christensen, A. (1988). Dysfunctional interaction patterns in couples. In P. Noller & M. A. Fitzpatrick (Eds.), *Perspectives on marital interaction* (pp. 31-52). Avon, UK: Multilingual Matters Press.

Christensen, A., & Heavey, C. L. (1990). Gender and social structure in the demand/withdraw pattern of marital conflict. *Journal of Personality and Social Psychology, 59,* 73-81.

Christensen, A., & Shenk, J. L. (1991). Communication, conflict, and psychological distance in nondistressed, clinic, and divorcing couples. *Journal of Consulting and Clinical Psychology, 59,* 458-463.

Christensen, A., & Walczynski, P. T. (1997). Conflict and satisfaction in couples. In R. J. Sternberg & M. Hojjat (Eds.), *Satisfaction in close relationships* (pp. 249-274). NY: Guilford Press.

Clark, R. D., & Hatfield, E. (1989). Gender differences in receptivity to sexual offers. *Journal of Psychology and Human Sexuality, 2,* 39-55.

Clements, M. L., Cordova, A. D., Markman, H. J., & Laurenceau, J. P. (1997). The erosion of marital satisfaction over time and how to prevent it. In R. J. Sternberg & M. Hojjat (Eds.) *Satisfaction in close relationships* (pp. 335-355). NY: Guilford Press.

Clements, M. L., Stanley, S. M., & Markman, H. J. (2004). Before they said "I do": Discriminating among marital outcomes over 13 years. *Journal of Marriage and the Family, 66,* 613-626.

Coan, J., Gottman, J. M., Babcock, J., & Jacobson, N. S. (1997). Battering and the male rejection of influence from women. *Aggressive Behavior, 23,* 375-388.

Cohn, D. (2013). *Love and marriage.* Washington, DC: Pew Research Center.

Cooper, J., & Scher, S. J. (1994). When do our actions affect our attitudes? In S. Shavitt & T. C. Brock (Eds.), *Persuasions* (pp. 95-112). Boston, MA: Allyn and Bacon.

Copeland, M. E., & McKay, M. (2002). *The depression workbook.* Oakland, CA: New Harbinger Publications.

Crosby, J. F. (1991). *Illusion and disillusion: The self in love and marriage* (4th ed.). Belmont, CA: Wadsworth Publishers.

Cross, S. E., & Morris, M. L. (2003). Getting to know you: The relational self-construal, relational cognition, and well-being. *Personality and Social Psychology Bulletin, 29,* 512-523.

Cowan, C. P., & Cowan, P. A. (1992). *When partners become parents: The big life change for couples.* NY: Basic Books.

Cox, F. D. (2011). *Human intimacy: Marriage, the family, and its meaning.* Belmont, CA: Wadsworth Publishing.

Cox, F.D., & Demmitt (2014). *Human Intimacy.* Belmont, CA: Wadsworth Publishing.

Creasy, G., & Jarvis, P. (2009). Attachment and marriage. In M. C. Smith & N. DeFrates-Densch (Eds.), *Handbook of research on adult learning and development* (pp. 269-304). NY: Routledge/Taylor and Francis.

Cross, S. E., Bacon, P. L., & Morris, M. L. (2000). The relational-independent self-construal and relationships. *Journal of Personality and Social Psychology, 78,* 791-808.

Cutrona, C. E. (1996). *Social support in couples.* Thousand Oaks, CA: Sage Publications.

Dattilia, F. M. (2010). *Cognitive-behavioral therapy with couples and families.* NY: Guilford.

Davies, S., Katz, J., & Jackson, J. L. (1999). Sexual desire discrepancies. *Archives of Sexual Behavior, 28,* 253- 271.

Davisson, J., & Davisson, K. (2010). Six keys to an outrageously happy marriage. In S. M. Alexander (Ed.), *All-in-one marriage prep* (pp. 318-322). Naples, FL: Barringer.

Deffenbacher, J. L. (1992). Trait anger: Theory, findings, and implications. In C. D. Spielberger & J. N. Butcher (Eds.), *Advances in personality assessment* (Vol. 9, pp. 177-201). Hillsdale, NJ: Lawrence Erlbaum.

DeGenova, M. K., (2008). *Intimate relationships, marriages, and families.* NY: McGraw-Hill.

DeGenova, M.K., Stinnett, N., & Stinnett, N. (2011). *Intimate Relationships*. NY: McGraw Hill.

Dehle, C., Larsen, D., & Landers, J. E. (2001). Social support in marriage. *American Journal of Family Therapy, 29,* 307-324.

Demaria, R., Hannah, M., & Gordon, L. H. (Eds.). (2002). *Building intimate relationships.* NY: Brunner-Routledge Publishers.

Devito, J. A. (2004). *Messages: Building interpersonal communication skills* (6th ed.). Boston, MA: Allyn and Bacon.

Dindia, K. (1994). A multiphasic view of relationship maintenance strategies. In D. J. Canary & L. Stafford (Eds.), *Communication and relational maintenance* (pp. 91-112). San Diego, CA: Academic Press.

Dindia, K. (2000). Relational maintenance. In S. S. Hendrick & C. Hendrick (Eds.), *Close relationships: A sourcebook* (pp. 287-299). Thousand Oaks, CA: Sage.

Dindia, K., & Canary, D. J. (Eds.) (1993). Relational maintenance [Special issue]. *Journal of Social and Personal Relationships, 10,* 163-304.

Doherty, W. J. (2013). *Take back your marriage: Sticking together in a world that pulls you apart.* NY: Guilford Press.

Duck, S. (1994). Steady as (s)he goes. In D. J. Canary & L. Stafford (Eds.), *Communication and relationship maintenance* (pp. 45-60). San Diego, CA: Academic Press.

Edelstein, R. S., & Shaver, P. R. (2004). Avoidant attachment: Exploration of an oxymoron. In A. P. Aron & D. J. Mashek (Eds.), *Handbook of closeness and intimacy* (pp. 397-412). Mahwah, NJ: Lawrence Erlbaum.

Edgar, D. (1999). Families as the crucible of competence in a changing social ecology. In E. Frydenberg (Ed.), *Learning to cope: Developing as a person in complex societies* (pp. 109-129). London: Oxford University Press.

Ehrenreich, B. (1987). *The hearts of men: American dreams and the flight from commitment.* Garden City, NY: Anchor Books.

Eldridge, K. A., & Baucom, B. (2012). Demand-withdraw communication in couples: Recent developments and future directions. In P. Noller & G. Karantzas (Eds.), *The Wiley-Blackwell handbook of couples and family relationships* (pp. 144-158).. Oxford, UK: Wiley-Blackwell.

Eldridge, K. A., Sevier, M., Jones, J., Atkins, D. C., & Christensen, A. (2007). Demand-withdraw communication in severely distressed, moderately distressed, and non-distressed couples. *Journal of Family Psychology, 21,* 218-226.

Emmons, W. A. (2007). *Thanks! How the new science of gratitude can make you happier.* NY: Houghton Mifflin.

Eshleman, J. R. (2003). *The family* (10th ed.). Boston, MA: Allyn and Bacon.

Eysenck, M. (2012). *Fundamentals of Cognition.* NY: Psychology Press

Fagan, P. F. (2009). *The effects of pornography on individuals, marriage, family, and community.* Washington, DC: Family Research Council.

Faludi, S. (2000). *Stiffed: The betrayal of the American man.* NY: William Morrow.

Family values: Belief in marriage and family life remains strong. (2002, Fall). *ISR SocialScience in the Public Interest, 2,* 1-2.

Fazio, R. (1987). Self-perception theory: A current perspective. In M. P. Zanna, J. M. Olson, & C. P. Herman (Eds.), *Ontario symposium on personality and social psychology* (pp. 129-150). Hillsdale, NJ: Lawrence Erlbaum.

Festinger, L. (1957). *A theory of cognitive dissonance.* Stanford, CA: Stanford University Press.

Fincham, F. D. (2000). The kiss of porcupines: From attributing responsibility to forgiving. *Personal Relationships, 7,* 1-23.

Fincham, F. D. (2004). Marital conflict: Correlates, structure, and context. In J. B. Ruscher & E.Y. Hammer (Eds.), *Current directions in social psychology* (pp. 83-90). Upper Saddle River, NJ: Prentice Hall.

Fincham, F. D., Beach, S. R. H., & Davila, J. (2004). Forgiveness and conflict resolution in marriage. *Journal of Family Psychology, 18,* 72-81.

Fincham, F. D., Paleari, G., & Regalia, C. (2002). Forgiveness in marriage: The role of relationship quality, attributions, and empathy. *Personal Relationships, 9,* 27-37.

Fincham, F. D., Stanley, S. M., & Beach, S. R. H. (2007). Transformational processes in marriage. *Journal of Marriage and Family, 69,* 275-292.

Finkel, E. J., Slotter, E. B., Luchies, L. B., Walton, G. M., & Gross, J. J. (2013). A brief intervention to promote conflict reappraisal preserves marital quality over time. *Psychological Science, 24,* 1595-1601.

Fitzpatrick, M. A. (1988). *Between husbands and wives: Communication in marriage.* Newbury Park, CA: Sage.

Fletcher, G. (2002). *The new science of intimate relationships.* Malden, MA; Blackwell Publishers.

Fowers, B. J. (2000). *Beyond the myth of marital happiness.* San Francisco, CA: Jossey-Bass.

Franz, C. M., & Seburn, M. (2003). Are argumentative people better or worse at seeing both sides? *Journal of Social and Personal Relationships, 20,* 565-573.

Fujishin, R. (1998). *Gifts from the heart: Ten communication skills for developing more loving relationships.* San Francisco, CA: Acada Books.

Gaelick, L., Bodenhausen, G. V., & Wyer, R. S. (1985). Emotional communication in close relationships. *Journal of Personality and Social Psychology, 49,* 1246-1265.

Gagne, F. M., & Lydon, J. E. (2003). Identification and the commitment shift: Accounting for gender differences in relationship illusions. *Personality and Social Psychology Bulletin, 29,* 907-919.

Gagne, F. M., & Lydon, J. E. (2004). Bias and accuracy in close relationships: An integrative review. *Personality and Social Psychology Review, 8,* 322-338.

Galvin, K.M., Bylund, C.L., & Brommel, B. (2011). *Family Communication.* NY: Allyn and Bacon.

Gigy, L., & Kelly, J. B. (1992). Reasons for divorce: Perspectives of divorcing men and women. *Journal of Divorce and Remarriage, 18,* 169-187.

Glass, L. (1992). *He says, she says: Closing the communication gap between the sexes.* NY: Perigee Books.

Glass, S. P. (2002). Couple therapy after the trauma of infidelity. In A. S. Gurman & N. S. Jacobson (Eds.), *Clinical handbook of couple therapy* (pp. 488-507). NY: Guilford Press.

Glass, S. P. (2003). *NOT "just friends."* NY: Free Press.

Glenn, N. D. (1996). Values, attitudes, and American marriage. In D. Popenoe, J. B. Elshtain, & D. Blankenhorn (Eds.), *Prom-*

ises to keep: Decline and renewal of marriage in America (pp. 15-33). Lantham, MD: Rowman and Littlefield Publishers.

Golomb, E. (1992). *Trapped in the mirror.* NY: Quill Publishers.

Gordon, K. C., Baucom, D. H., & Snyder, D. K. (2000). The use of forgiveness in marital therapy. In M. E. McCullough, K. I. Pargament, & C. E. Thoresen (Eds.), *Forgiveness:Theory, research, and practice* (pp. 203-227). NY: Guilford Press.

Gottman, J. M. (1979). *Marital interactions: Experimental investigations.* NY: Academic Press.

Gottman, J. M. (1993). The roles of conflict engagement, escalation, or avoidance in marital interaction: A longitudinal view of five types of couples. *Journal of Consulting and Clinical Psychology, 61,* 1-15.

Gottman, J. M. (1994a). *What predicts divorce? The relationship between marital processes and marital outcomes.* Hillsdale, NJ: Lawrence Erlbaum.

Gottman, J. M. (1994b). Why marriages fail. *Family Therapy Networker* (May/June), 40-48.

Gottman, J. M. (1994c). *Why marriages succeed or fail...and how you can make yours last.* NY: Simon and Schuster.

Gottman, J. M. (1999). *The marriage clinic: A scientifically-based marital therapy.* NY: Norton Publications.

Gottman, J. M. (2011). *The science of trust.* NY: Norton.

Gottman, J. M., & Carrere, S. (1994). Why can't men and women get along? Developmental roots and marital inequalities. In D. J. Canary & L. Stafford (Eds.), *Communication and relational maintenance* (pp. 203-229). San Diego, CA: Academic Press.

Gottman, J. M., Coan, J., Carrere, S., & Swanson, C. (1998). Predicting marital happiness and stability from newlywed interactions. *Journal of Marriage and the Family, 60,* 5-22.

Gottman, J. M., & DeClaire, J. (2002). *The relationship cure.* NY: Crown Publishers.

Gottman, J. M., & Krokoff, L. J. (1989). Marital interaction and satisfaction: A longitudinal view. *Journal of Consulting and Clinical Psychology, 57,* 47-52.

Gottman, J. M., & Levenson, R. W. (1999). What predicts change in marital interaction over time? A study of alternative models. *Family Process, 38,* 143-158.

Gottman, J. M., & Levenson, R. W. (2000). The timing of divorce: Predicting when a couple will divorce over a 14-year period. *Journal of the Family, 62,* 737-745.

Gottman, J. M., & Levenson, R. W. (2002). A two-factor model for predicting when a couple will divorce: Exploratory analyses using 14-year longitudinal data. *Family Process, 41,* 83-97.

Gottman, J. M., & Notarius, C. I. (2000). Decade review: Observing marital interaction. *Journal of Marriage and the Family, 62,* 927-947.

Gottman, J. M., & Notarius, C. I. (2002). Marital research in the 20th century and a research agenda for the 21st century. *Family Process, 41,* 159-198.

Gottman, J. M., Notarius, C. I., Gonso, J., & Markman, H. J. (1976). *A couple's guide to communication.* Champaign, IL: Research Press.

Gottman, J. M., & Silver, N. (1999). *The seven principles for making marriage work.* NY: Three Rivers Press.

Gottman, J. M., & Silver, N. (2012). *What makes love last.* NY: Simon and Schuster.

Goulston, M., & Goldberg, P. (2002). *The six secrets of a lasting relationship.* NY: Putnam.

Gray, J. (2012). *Men are from Mars, women are from Venus.* NY: Harper.

Gray-Little, B., Baucom, D. H., & Hamby, S. L. (1996). Marital power, marital adjustment, and therapy outcome. *Journal of Family Process, 10,* 292-303.

Greeff, A. P., & Malherbe, H. L. (2001). Intimacy and marital satisfaction in spouses. *Journal of Sex and Marital Therapy, 27,* 247-257.

Guldner, G. T. (1996). Long-distance romantic relationships: Prevalence and separation-related symptoms in college students. *Journal of College Student Development, 37,* 289-296.

Gutierres, S. E., Kenrick, D. T., & Partch, J. J. (1999). Beauty, dominance, and the mating game: Contrast effects in self-assessment reflect gender differences. *Personality and Social Psychology Bulletin, 25,* 1126-1134.

Halpern, H. M. (2003). *How to break your addiction to a person.* NY: Bantam Books.

Halpern, H. M. (2005). *Cutting loose.* NY: Fireside. (2003). *Hardwired to Connect.* NY: Institute

Harley, W. F. (2001). *Fall in love, stay in love.* Grand Rapids, MI: Revell.

Harley, W. F. (2009). *Five steps to romantic love.* Grand Rapids, MI: Revell.

Hawkins, M. W., Carrere, S., & Gottman, J. M. (2002). Marital sentiment override: Does it influence couples' perceptions? *Journal of Marriage and the Family, 64,* 193-201.

Heaton, T. B., & Blake, A. M. (1999). Gender differences in determinants of marital disruption. *Journal of Family Issues, 20,* 25-45.

Heavey, C. L., Christensen, A., & Malamuth, N. M. (1995). The longitudinal impact of demand and withdraw during marital conflict. *Journal of Consulting and Clinical Psychology, 63,* 797-801.

Heavey, C. L., Layne, C., & Christensen, A. (1993). Gender and conflict structure in marital interaction: A replication and extension. *Journal of Consulting and Clinical Psychology, 61,* 16-27.

Helgeson, V. S., Shaver, P., & Dyer, M. (9187). Prototypes of intimacy and distance in same-sex and opposite-sex relationships. *Journal of Social and Personal Relationships, 4,* 195-273.

Hightower, N. (2002). *Anger busting 101: The new ABCs for angry men and the women who love them.* Houston, TX: Bayou Publishers.

Hogan, E. E., & Hogan, S. (2000). *Intellectual foreplay.* Alameda, CA: Hunter House Publishers.

Holley, S. R., Haase, C. M., & Levenson, R. W. (2013). Age-related changes in demand-withdraw communication patterns. *Journal of Marriage and Family, 75,* 822-836.

Holtzworth-Munroe, A., & Stuart, G. L. (1994). The relationship standards and assumptions of violent and non-violent husbands. *Cognitive Therapy and Research, 18,* 87-104.

Howell, P., & Jones, R. (2010). *World class marriage: How to create the relationship you always wanted with the partner you already have.* NY: Rowman and Littlefield.

Huston, T. L., Caughlin, J. P., Houts, R. M., Smith, S. E., & George, L. J. (2001). The connubial crucible: Newlywed years as predictors of marital delight, distress, and divorce. *Journal of Personality and Social Psychology, 80,* 237-252.

Huston, T. L., & Chorost, A. F. (1994). Behavioral buffers on the effects of negativity on marital satisfaction: A longitudinal study. *Personal Relationships, 1,* 223-239.

Huston, T. L., & Geis, G. (1993). In what ways do gender-related attributes and beliefs affect marriage? *Journal of Social Issues, 49,* 87-106.

Huston, T. L., & Houts, R. M. (1998). The psychological infrastructure of courtship and marriage: The role of personality and compatibility in romantic relationships. In T. N. Bradbury (Ed.), *The developmental course of marital dysfunction* (pp. 114-151). Cambridge, UK: Cambridge University Press.

Huston, T. L., McHale, S. M., & Crouter, A. C. (1986). When the honeymoon's over: Changes in the marriage relationship over the first year. In R. Gilmour & S. Duck (Eds.), *The emerging field of personal relationships* (pp. 109-132). Hillsdale, NJ: Lawrence Erlbaum.

Huston, T. L., Niehuis, S., & Smith, S. E. (2001). The early marital roots of conjugal distress and divorce. *Current Directions in Psychological Science, 10,* 116-119.

Huston, T. L., & Vangelisti, A. L. (1991). Socioemotional behavior and satisfaction in marital relationships: A longitudinal study. *Journal of Personality and Social Psychology, 61,* 721-733.

Hyde, J. S. (2005). The gender similarities hypothesis. *American Psychologist, 60,* 581-592.

Infante, D. A., & Rancer, A. S. (1982). A conceptualization and measure of argumentativeness. *Journal of Personality Assessment, 46,* 72-80.

Ireland, J. L. (2002). How does assertiveness relate to bullying behavior among prisoners? *Legal and Criminological Psychology, 7,* 87-100.

Jacobson, N. S. (1989). The maintenance of treatment gains following social learning-based marital therapy. *Behavior Therapy, 20,* 325-336.

Janda, L. (1996). *The psychologist's book of self-tests.* NY: Perigee Books.

Johnson, A. F. (2003). Multiple role self-efficacy and value attainment: Personal factors that mediate the relationships between levels of work and family involvement and work-family conflict. *Dissertation Abstracts International, 64,* 3B. (UMI No. 1494)

Johnson, D. J., & Rusbult, C. E. (1989). Resisting temptation: Devaluation of alternative partners as a means of maintaining commitment in close relationships. *Journal of Personality and Social Psychology, 57,* 967-980.

Johnson, F. L. (1996). Friendships among women: Closeness in dialogue. In J. T. Wood (Ed.), *Gendered relationships* (pp. 79-94). Mountain View, CA: Mayfield Publishers.

Johnson, M. D. (2002). The observation of specific affect in marital interactions: Psychometric properties of a coding system and a rating system. *Psychological Assessment, 14,* 423-438.

Johnson, M. D., Cohan, C. L., Davila, J., Lawrence, E., Rogge, R. D., Karney, B. R., Sullivan, K. T., & Bradbury, T. N. (2005). Problem-solving skills and affective expressions as predictors of change in marital satisfaction. *Journal of Consulting and Clinical Psychology, 73,* 15-27.

Jones, S. M., & Burleson, B. R. (1997). The impact of situational variables on helpers' perceptions of comforting messages: An attributional analysis. *Communication Research, 24,* 530-555.

Jones, S. M., & Burleson, B. R. (2003). Effects of helper and recipient sex on the experience and outcomes of comforting messages: An experimental investigation. *Sex roles, 48,* 1-19.

Jordan, J. V. (1991). *Women's growth in connection.* NY: Guilford Publishers. Kantrowitz, B., & Wingert, P. (2002). The science of a good marriage. In K. R. Gilbert (Ed.), *Annual editions: The family* (pp. 84-87). Guilford, CT: McGraw-Hill/Dushkin.

Karney, B. R., & Bradbury, T. N. (1995). The longitudinal course of marital quality and stability: A review of theory, method, and research. *Psychological Bulletin, 118,* 3-34.

Karney, B. R., & Bradbury, T. N. (1997). Neuroticism, marital interaction, and the trajectory of marital satisfaction. *Journal of Personality and Social Psychology, 72,* 1075-1092.

Karney, B. R., & Bradbury, T. N. (2000). Attributions in marriage: State or trait? A growth curve analysis. *Journal of Personality and Social Psychology, 78,* 295-309.

Kayser, K. (1993). *When love dies: The process of marital disaffection.* NY: Guilford Press.

Kayser, K., & Himle, D. P. (2002). Dysfunctional beliefs about intimacy. In R. L. Leahy & E. T. Dowd (Eds.), *Clinical advances in cognitive psychotherapy* (pp. 361-376). NY: Springer Publications.

Kelly, J. B. (1982). Divorce: The adult perspective. In B. B. Wolman & G. Stricker (Eds.), *Handbook of developmental psychology* (pp. 734-750). Englewood Cliffs, NJ: Prentice Hall.

Kenrick, D. T., & Gutierres, S. E. (1980). Contrast effects and judgments of physical attractiveness: When beauty becomes a social problem. *Journal of Personality and Social Psychology, 38,* 131-140.

Kenrick, D. T., Gutierres, S. E., & Goldberg, L. L. (1989). Influence of popular erotica on judgments of strangers and mates. *Journal of Experimental Social Psychology, 25,* 159-167.

Kenrick, D. T., Neuberg, S. L., Zierk, K. L., & Krones, J. M. (1994). Evolution and social cognition: Contrast effects as a function of sex, dominance, and physical attractiveness. *Personality and Social Psychology Bulletin, 20,* 210-217.

Kiley, D. (1983). *The Peter Pan syndrome: Men who have never grown up.* NY: Avon Books.

Kimmel, M. (1996). *Manhood in America: A cultural history.* NY: Free Press.

Klinetob, N. A., & Smith, D. A. (1996). Demand-withdraw communication in marital interaction: Tests of interspousal contingency and gender role hypotheses. *Journal of Marriage and the Family, 58,* 945-957.

Knight, B. (2002). *Knight: My story.* NY: Thomas Dunne Books.

Knox, D., & Schacht, C. (2012). *Choices in relationships: An introduction to marriage and the family.* Belmont, CA: Wadsworth Publishers.

Krokoff, L. J. (1987). The correlates of negative affect in marriage: An exploratory study of gender differences. *Journal of Family Issues, 8,* 111-135.

Krokoff, L. J. (1990). Hidden agendas in marriage: Affective and longitudinal dimensions. *Communication Research, 17,* 483-499.

Kunkel, A. W., & Burleson, B. R. (1998). Social support and the emotional lives of men and women: An assessment of the different cultures perspective. In D. J. Canary & K. Dindia

(Eds.), *Sex differences and similarities in communication: Critical essays and empirical investigations of sex and gender in interaction* (pp. 101-125). Mahwah, NJ: Lawrence Erlbaum.

Kunkel, A. W., & Burleson, B. R. (1999). Assessing explanations for sex differences in emotional support: A test of the different cultures and skill specialization accounts. *Human Communication Research, 25,* 307-340.

Kupers, T. A. (1993). *Revisioning men's lives: Gender, intimacy, and power.* NY: Guilford Press.

Kurdek, L. A. (1999). The nature and predictors of the trajectory of change in marital quality for husbands and wives over the first 10 years of marriage. *Developmental Psychology, 35,* 1283-1296.

Kyratzis, A. (2001). Children's gender indexing in language: From the separate worlds hypothesis to considerations of culture, context, and power. *Research on Language and Social Interaction, 34,* 1-13.

Lambert, N. M., Negash, S., Stillman, T. F., Olmstead, S. B., & Fincham, F. D. (2012). A love that doesn't last: Pornography consumption and weakened commitment to one's romantic partner. *Journal of Social and Clinical Psychology, 31,* 410-438.

Lamanna, M. A., Riedmann, A., & Stewart, S. D. (2014). *Marriage and families: Making choices in a diverse society.* Belmont, CA: Wadsworth Publishers.

Lauer, R. H., & Lauer, J. C. (2009). *Marriage and family: A quest for intimacy.* NY: McGraw Hill.

Laurenceau, J. P., Barrett, L. F., & Pietromonoca, P. R. (1998). Intimacy as an interpersonal process: The importance of self-disclosure, partner disclosure, and perceived partner responsiveness in interpersonal exchanges. *Journal of Personality and Social Psychology, 74,* 1238-1251.

Leiter, M. P., & Durup, M. J. (1996). Work, home, and in-between: A longitudinal study of spillover. *Journal of Applied Behavioral Science, 32,* 29-47.

Lemasters, E. E. (1957). Parenthood as a crisis. *Marriage and Family Living, 19,* 352-355.

Levant, R. F. (1995). *Masculinity reconstructed: Changing the rules of manhood at work, in relationships, and in family life.* NY: Dutton and Dutton.

Levenson, R. W., & Gottman, J. M. (1985). Physiological and affective predictors of change in relationship satisfaction. *Journal of Personality and Social Psychology, 49,* 85-94.

Lewis, C. S. (2009). *The Screwtape Letters (reprint ed.).* NY: Harper One.

Love, P. (2001). *The Truth About Love.* NY: Fireside.

Lower, L. M. (2005). Couples with young children. In M. Harway (Ed.), *Handbook of couples therapy* (pp. 44-60). NY: Wiley.

Maccoby, E.E. (1988). Gender as a social category. *Developmental Psychology, 26,* 755-765.

Maccoby, E. E. (1990). Gender and relationships: A development account. *American Psychologist, 45,* 513-520.

MacGeorge, E. L., Graves, A. R., Feng, B., Gillihan, S. J., & Burleson, B. R. (2004). The myth of gender cultures: Similarities outweigh differences in men's and women's provision of and responses to supportive communication. *Sex Roles, 50,* 143-175.

Mahoney, A., Pargament, K. I., Tarakeshwar, N., & Swank, A. B. (2008). Religion in the home in the 1980s and 1990s: A meta-analytic review and conceptual analysis of links between religion, marriage, and parenting. *Psychology of Religion and Spirituality, 5,* 63-101.

Malamuth, N. M. (1984). Aggression against women: Cultural and individual causes. In N. M. Malamuth & E. Donnerstein (Eds.), *Pornography and sexual aggression* (pp. 19-52). Orlando, FL: Academic Press.

Maltz, D. N., & Borker, R. A. (1982). A cultural approach to male-female miscommunication. In J. J. Gumperz (Ed.), *Language and social identity* (pp. 196-216). Cambridge: Cambridge University Press.

Maltz, W., & Maltz, L. (2008). *The porn trap.* NY: Collins.

Manning, J. C. (2006). The impact of internet pornography on marriage and the family: A review of the research. *Sexual Addiction and Compulsivity, 13,* 131-165.

Margolin, G., & Wampold, B. (1981). Sequential analysis of conflict and accord in distressed and nondistressed marital partners. *Journal of Consulting and Clinical Psychology, 49,* 554-567.

Markman, H. J. (1991). Constructive marital conflict is NOT an oxymoron. *Behavioral Assessment, 13,* 83-96.

Markman, H. J., & Kraft, S. A. (1989). Men and women in marriage: Dealing with gender differences in marital therapy. *Behavior Therapist, 12,* 51-56.

Markman, H., Stanley, S., & Blumberg, S. L. (1994). *Fighting for your marriage.* San Francisco, CA: Jossey-Bass Publishers.

Markman, H., Stanley, S., & Blumberg, S. L. (2010). *Fighting for your marriage (revised ed.).* San Francisco, CA: Jossey-Bass.

Martz, J. M., Verette, J., Arriaga, S. B., Slovik, L. F., Cox, C. L., & Rusbult, C. E. (1998). Positive illusions in close relationships. *Personal Relationships, 5,* 159-181.

Mashek, D. J., & Sherman, M. D. (2004). Desiring less closeness with intimate others. In A. P. Aron & D. J. Mashek (Eds.), *Handbook of closeness and intimacy* (pp. 343-356). Mahwah, NJ: Lawrence Erlbaum.

Masuda, M., & Duck, S. (2002). Issues in ebb and flow: Management and maintenance of relationships as a skilled activity. In A. Wenzel & J. H. Harvey (Eds.), *A clinician's guide to maintaining and enhancing close relationships* (pp. 827-842). Mahweh, NJ: Lawrence Erlbaum.

Matthews, L. S., Wickrama, K. A. S., & Conger, R. D. (1996). Predicting marital instability from spouse and observer reports of marital interaction. *Journal of Marriage and the Family, 58,* 641-655.

McCarthy, B. (1999). Martial style and its effects on sexual desire and functioning. *Journal of Family Psychotherapy, 10,* 1-12.

McCarthy, B. (2001). Marital sex as it ought to be. *Journal of Family Psychotherapy, 14,* 1-12.

McCarthy, B., & McCarthy, E. (1992). *Intimate marriage.* NY: Carroll and Graf Publishers.

McCarthy, B., & McCarthy, E. (2003). *Rekindling desire: A step-by-step program to help low -sex and no-sex marriages.* NY: Brunner-Routledge.

McCullough, M. E., Rachal, K. C., Sandage, S. J., Worthington, Jr., E. L., Brown, S. W., & Hight, T. L. (1998). Interpersonal forgiving in close relationships: Theoretical elaboration and measurement. *Journal of Personality and Social Psychology, 75,* 1586-1603.

McFarlane, E., & Saywell, J. (1998). *If questions for the soul.* NY: Villard Publications.

McGonagle, K. A., Kessler, R. C., & Gotlib, I. H. (1993). The effects of marital disagreement style, frequency, and outcome on marital disruption. *Journal of Social and Personal Relationships, 10,* 385-404.

McKay, M., Davis, M., & Fanning, P. (1981). *Thoughts and feelings: The art of cognitive stress intervention.* Oakland, CA: New Harbinger Publications.

McKay, M., Davis, M., & Fanning, P. (2009). *Messages: The communication skills book.* Oakland, CA: New Harbinger Publications.

McKay, M., Davis, M., & Fanning, P. (2011). *Thought and feelings: Taking control of your moods and your life.* Oakland, CA: New Harbinger Publications.

McKay, M., Fanning, P., & Paleg, K. (2006). *Couple skills: Making your relationship work.* Oakland, CA: New Harbinger Publications.

McKay, M., Rogers, P. D., & McKay, J. (1989). *When anger hurts.* Oakland, CA: New Harbinger Publications.

McNulty, J. K., & Karney, B. R. (2001). Attributions in marriage: Integrating specific and global evaluations of a relationship. *Personality and Social Psychology Bulletin, 27,* 943-955.

Mehrabian, A. (1981). *Silent messages: Implicit communication of emotion and attitudes* (2nd ed.). Belmont, CA: Wadsworth.

Melamed, L., & Moss, M. K. (1975). The effect of context on ratings of attractiveness of photographs. *Journal of Psychology, 90,* 129-136.

Mellody, P., & Freundlich, L. S. (2003). *The intimacy factor: The ground rules for overcoming the obstacles to truth, respect, and lasting love.* San Francisco, CA: Harper.

Monsour, M. (1992). Meanings of intimacy in cross- and same-sex friendships. *Journal of Social and Personal Relationships, 9,* 277-296.

Mulliken, T. (1998). *The state of affairs: Why they happen and how love can be restored.* Mukilteo, WA: Wine Press Publishing.

Murray, S. L. (1999). The quest for conviction: Motivated cognition in romantic relationships. *Psychological Inquiry, 10,* 23-34.

Murray, S. L., & Holmes, J. G. (1997). A leap of faith? Positive illusions in romantic relationships. *Personality and Social Psychology Bulletin, 23,* 586-604.

Murray, S. L., Holmes, J. G., & Griffin, D. W. (1996). The self-fulfilling nature of positive illusions in romantic relationships: Love is not blind but prescient. *Journal of Personality and Social Psychology, 71,* 1155-1180.

Neff, L. A., & Karney, B. R. (2005). To know you is to love you: The implications of global adoration and specific accuracy for marital relationships. *Journal of Personality and Social Psychology, 88,* 480-497.

Newell, W. (2003). *The code of man: Love courage pride family country.* NY: Regan Books.

Nicholaus, B., & Lowrie, P. (2000). *The conversation piece 2.* NY: Ballantine Books.

Nichols, M. P., & Schwartz, R. C. (2003). *Family therapy: Concepts and methods* (6th ed.). Needham Heights, MA: Allyn and Bacon.

Noller, P. (1984). *Nonverbal communication and marital interaction.* Elmsford, NY: Pergamon.

Noller, P. (1993). Gender and emotional communication in marriage: Different cultures or differential social power? *Journal of Language and Social Psychology, 12,* 132-152.

Noller, P., & Feeney, J. A. (1998). Communication in early marriage: Responses to conflict, nonverbal accuracy, and conversational patterns. In T. N. Bradbury (Ed.), *The developmental course of marital dysfunction* (pp. 11-43). Cambridge, UK: Cambridge University Press.

Norcross, J. C., Santrock, J. W., Campbell, L. F., Smith, T. P., Sommer, R., & Zuckerman, E. L. (2003). *Authoritative guide to self-help resources in mental health* (revised ed.). NY: Guilford Press.

Notarius, C. I., Benson, P. R., Sloane, D., Vanzetti, N. A., & Hornyak, L. M. (1989). Exploring the interface between perception and behavior: An analysis of marital interaction in distressed and nondistressed couples. *Behavioral Assessment, 11,* 39-64.

Notarius, C. I., & Johnson, J. (1982). Emotional expression in husbands and wives. *Journal of Marriage and the Family, 44,* 483-489.

Notarius, C. I., & Markman, H. (1993). *We can work it out: Making sense out of marital conflict.* NY: Putnam Publications.

Notarius, C. I., & Pelligrini, D. S. (1987). Differences between husbands and wives: implications for understanding marital discord. In K. Hahlweg & M. Goldstein (Eds.), *Understanding major mental disorder: The contribution of family interaction research* (pp. 231-249). NY: Family Process Press.

Olson, D. H., & DeFrain, J. (2003). *Marriages and families: Intimacy, diversity, and strengths.* NY: McGraw-Hill Publishers.

Olson, D. H., DeFrain, J., & Skogrand, L. (2011). *Marriages and Families.* NY: McGraw Hill.

Olson, D. H., & Olson, A. K. (2000). *Empowering couples: Building on your strengths.* Minneapolis, MN: Life Innovations.

Oltmanns, T. F., & Emery, R. E. (2004). *Abnormal psychology* (4th ed.). Upper Saddle River, NJ: Prentice Hall.

Owens, E. W., Behun, R. J., Manning, J. C., & Reid, R. C. (2012). The impact of internet pornography on adolescents: A review of the research. *Sexual Addiction and Compulsivity, 19,* 99-122.

Paloutzian, R.F., & Park, C.L. (2013). Handbook of the Psychology of Religion and Spirituality. NY: Guilford.

Parker-Pope, T. (2010). *For better: The science of a good marriage.* NY: Dutton.

Pasch, L. A., & Bradbury, T. N. (1998). Social support, conflict, and the development of marital dysfunction. *Journal of Consulting and Clinical Psychology, 66,* 219-230.

Patz, A. (2002). Will your marriage last? In K. R. Gilbert (Ed.), *Annual editions: The family* (pp. 88-92). Guilford, CT: McGraw-Hill/Dushkin.

Payson, E. (2002). *The wizard of Oz and other narcissists: Coping with the one-way relationship in work, love, and family.* NY: Julian Day Publications.

Peplau, L. A. (2004). Human sexuality: How do men and women differ? In J. A. Ruscher & E. Y. Hammer (Eds.), *Current directions in social psychology* (pp. 76-82). Upper Saddle River, NJ: Prentice Hall.

Perry-Jenkins, M., Repetti, R. L., & Crouter, A. C. (2000). Work and family in the 1990s. *Journal of Marriage and the Family, 62,* 981-998.

Persons, J. B. (1989). *Cognitive therapy in practice: A case formulation approach.* NY: Norton.

Piorkowski, G. K. (1994). *Too close for comfort: Exploring the risks of intimacy.* NY: Plenum Press.

Piver, S. (2000). *The hard questions.* NY: Putnam Publications.

Pittman, F. S. (1993). *Man enough: Fathers, sons, and the search for masculinity.* NY: Putnam Publishers.

Pittman, F. (1997). Just in love. *Journal of Marital and Family Therapy, 23,* 309-312.

Pittman, F. (1998). *Grow up! How taking responsibility can make you a happy adult.* NY: Golden Books.

Pollman-Schult, M. (2014). Parenthood and life satisfaction. *Journal of Marriage and Family, 76,* 319-336.

Popenoe, D. (1996). *Life without father.* Cambridge, MA: Harvard University Press.

Popenoe, D., & Whitehead, B. D. (1999). The state of our unions: The social health of marriage in America. *The National Marriage Project.* New Brunswick, NJ: Rutgers University.

Prager, K. J., & Roberts, L. J. (2004). Deep intimate connection: Self and intimacy in couple relationships. In A. P. Aron & D. J. Machek (Eds.), *Handbook of closeness and intimacy* (pp. 43-60). Mahwah, NJ: Lawrence Erlbaum.

Prochaska, J. O., Norcross, J. C., & DiClemente, C. C. (1994). *Changing for good: A revolutionary six-stage program for overcoming bad habits and moving your life positively forward.* NY: Avon Books.

Ragsdale, J. D. (1996). Gender, satisfaction level, and the use of relational maintenance strategies in marriage. *Communication Monographs, 63,* 354-369.

Reid, D. E., Dalton, J., Laderoute, K., Doell, F. K., & Hguyen, T. (2006). Therapeutically-induced changes in couple identity: The role of we-ness and interpersonal processing in relationship satisfaction. *Genetic, Social, and General Psychology Monographs, 132,* 241-284.

Raush, H. L., Barry, W. A., Hertel, R. K., & Swain, M. A. (1974). *Communication, conflict, and marriage.* San Francisco, CA: Jossey-Bass.

Reik, T. (1976). *Of love and lust.* NY: Pyramid Books.

Reis, H. T. (1998). Gender differences in intimacy and related behaviors: Context and process. In D. J. Canary & K. Dindia (Eds.), *Sex differences and similarities in communication: Critical essays and empirical investigations of sex and gender in intimacy* (pp. 203-231). Mahwah, NJ: Lawrence Erlbaum.

Reis, H. T., & Patrick, B. C. (1996). Attachment and intimacy: Component processes. In E. T. Higgins & A. W. Kruglanski (Eds.), *Social psychology: Handbook of basic principles* (pp. 523-563). NY: Guilford Press.

Reis, H. T., Senchak, M., & Solomon, B. (1985). Sex differences in the intimacy of social interactions: Further examination of potential explanations. *Journal of Personality and Social Psychology, 48,* 1204-1217.

Robbins, R. W., & Beer, J. S. (2001). Positive illusions about the self: Short-term benefits and long-term costs. *Journal of Personality and Social Psychology, 80,* 340-352.

Roberts, L. J. (2000). Fire and ice in marital communication: Hostile and distancing behaviors as predictors of marital distress. *Journal of Marriage and the Family, 62,* 693-707.

Roberts, N. C., & Levenson, R. W. (2001). The remains of the workday: Impact of job stress and exhaustion on marital interaction in police couples. *Journal of Marriage and the Family, 63,* 1052-1067.

Robinson, J. (2012). *Communication Miracles for Couples: Easy and Effective Tools to Create More Love and Less Conflict.* Newburyport, MA: Conari Press.

Roper Center Data Review. (1998). The family: Marriage: Highly valued. *The Public Perspective, 9,* 17.

Rugel, R. P. (1997). *Husband-focused marital therapy: An approach to dealing with marital distress.* Springfield, IL: Charles C. Thomas Publishers.

Rusbult, C. E., Verette, J., Whitney, G. A., Slovik, L. F., & Lipkus, I. (1991). Accommodation processes in close relationships: Theory and preliminary empirical evidence. *Journal of Personality and Social Psychology, 60,* 53-78.

Sagrestano, L. M., Christensen, A., & Heavey, C. L. (1998). Social influence techniques during marital conflict. *Personal Relationships, 5,* 75-89.

Sagrestano, L. M., Heavey, C. L., & Christensen, A. (1998). Theoretical approaches to understanding sex differences and similarities in conflict behavior. In D. J. Canary & K. Dindia (Eds.), *Sex differences and similarities in communication* (pp. 287-302). Mahwah, NJ: Lawrence Erlbaum.

Saitzyk, A. R., Floyd, F. J., & Kroll, A. B. (1997). Sequential analysis of autonomy- interdependence and affiliation-disaffiliation in couples' social support interactions. *Personal Relationships, 4,* 341-360.

Sax, L. (2007). *Boys Adrift.* NY: Basic Books.

Schaeffer, B. (2009). *Is it love or is it addiction?* Center City, MN: Hazeldon Press.

Schilling, E. A., Baucom, D. H., Burnett, C. K., Allen, E. S., & Ragland, L. (2003). Altering the course of marriage. *Journal of Family Psychology, 17,* 41-53.

Schnarch, D. (1997). *Passionate marriage.* NY: Norton.

Schnarch, D. (2001). The therapist in the crucible. In S. H. McDaniel, D. D Lusterman, & C. L. Philpot (Eds.), *Casebook for integrating family therapy: An ecosystemic approach* (pp. 43-56). Washington, DC: American Psychological Association.

Schneider, J. P. (2000). Effects of cybersex addiction on the family: Results of a survey. *Sexual Addiction and Compulsivity, 7,* 31-58.

Schneider, S. L. (2001). In search of realistic optimism: Meaning, knowledge, and warm fuzziness. *American Psychologist, 56,* 250-263.

Schwartz, M. A., & Scott, B. M. (2012). *Marriages and families: Diversity and change.* Upper Saddle River, NJ: Prentice-Hall.

Scott, S. B., Rhoades, G. K., Stanley, S. M., Allen, E. S., & Markman, H. J. (2013). Reasons for divorce and recollections of premarital intervention. *Couple and Family Psychology: Research and Practice, 2,* 131-145.

Seccombe, K., & Warner, R. L. (2004). *Marriages and families.* Belmont, CA: Wadsworth.

Seider, B. H., Hirschberger, G., Nelson, K. L., & Levenson, R. W. (2009). We can work it out. *Psychology and Aging, 24,* 604-613.

Shaver, P. R., & Hazan, C. (1993). Adult romantic attachment: Theory and evidence. In W. H. Jones & D. Perlman (Eds.), *Advances in personal relationships* (Vol. 4, pp. 29-70). London: Jessica Kingleys Publishers.

Smilek, D., Sinnett, S., & Kingstone, A. (2013). *Cognition.* NY: Oxford University Press.

Smith, D. A., Vivian, D., & O'Leary, K. D. (1990). Longitudinal prediction of marital discord from premarital expressions of affect. *Journal of Consulting and Clinical Psychology, 58,* 790-798.

Sprecher, S. (2002). Sexual satisfaction in premarital relationships: Associations with satisfaction, love, commitment, and stability. *The Journal of Sex Research, 39,* 190-196.

Spilka, B., Hood, R. W., Hunsberger, B., & Gorsuch, R. (2009). *The psychology of religion.* NY: Guilford.

Sprecher, S., Metts, S., Burleson, B., Hatfield, E., & Thompson, A. (1995). Domains of expressive interaction in intimate relationships: Associations with satisfaction and commitment. *Family Relations, 44,* 1-8.

Stafford, L., & Canary, D.J. (2006). *Equity and Interdependence as Predictors of Relational Maintenance Strategies. Journal of Family Communication, 6,* 227-254.

Stanley, S. M. (2005). *The power of commitment.* San Francisco, CA: Jossey-Bass.

Stanley, S. M., Markman, H. J., & Whitton, S. W. (2002). Communication, conflict, and commitment: Insights on the foundations of relationship success from a national survey. *Family Process, 41,* 659-676.

Sternberg, R. J. (1988). *The triangle of love: Intimacy, passion, and commitment.* NY: Basic Books.

Sternberg, R. J. (1991). *Love the way you want it.* NY: Bantam Books.

Streff, C. E. (1994). Humor in family therapy: Laughter in the crucible. In E. S. Buchman (Ed.), *The handbook of humor: Clinical applications in psychotherapy* (pp. 91-101). Melbourne, FL: Robert E. Krieger Publishers.

Strepp, L.S. (2007). *Unhooked.* NY: Riverhead Books.

Stock, G. (1987). *The book of questions.* NY: Workman Publishing.

Strong, B., & Cohen, T. F. (2013). *The Marriage and Family Experience.* Boston, MA: Cengage.

Strong, B., DeVault, C., & Sayad, B. W. (2003). *The marriage and family experience: Intimate relationships in a changing society* (8th ed.). Belmont, CA: Wadsworth Publishing.

Struthers, W. M. (2009). *Wired for intimacy: How pornography hijacks the male brain.* NY: IVP Press.

Tannen, D. (1990). *You just don't understand: Women and men in conversation.* New York: William Morrow Publishers.

Tannen, D. (2007). *You just don't understand: Women and men in conversation (revised ed.).* NY: William Morrow Publishers.

Tavris, C. (1989). *Anger: The misunderstood emotion.* NY: Simon and Schuster.

Terman, L. M., Buttenweiser, P., Ferguson, L. W., Johnson, W. B., & Wilson, D. P. (1938). *Psychological factors in marital happiness.* NY: McGraw-Hill.

Tidwell, M. O., Reis, H. T., & Shaver, P. R. (1996). Attachment, attractiveness, and social interactions: A diary study. *Journal of Personality and Social Psychology, 71,* 729-745.

Twenge, J. M., Campbell, W. K., & Foster, C. A. (2003). Parenthood and marital satisfaction: A meta-analytic review. *Journal of Marriage and the Family, 65,* 574-583.

Vangelisti, A. L. (1997). Gender differences, similarities, and interdependencies: Some problems with the different cultures perspective. *Personal Relationships, 4,* 243-253.

Vangelisti, A. L., Corbin, S. D., Luechetti, A. E., & Sprague, R. J. (1999). Couples' concurrent cognitions. *Human Communication Research, 25,* 370-398.

Vanletisti, A. L., & Daly, J. A. (1999). Gender differences in standards for romantic relationships: Different cultures or different experiences? In L. A. Peplau, S. C. Debro, R. C. Veniegas, & P. L. Taylor (Eds.), *Gender, culture, and ethnic-*

ity: Current research about women and men (pp. 182-199). Mountain View, CA: Mayfield Publishing.

Vangelisti, A. L., & Huston, T. L. (1994). Maintaining marital satisfaction and love. In D. J. Canary & L. Stafford (Eds.), *Communication and relational maintenance* (pp. 165-186). San Diego, CA: Academic Press.

Van Horn, R. K., Arnone, A., Nesbitt, K., Desilets, L., Sears, T., Giffin, M., & Brudi, R. (1997). Physical distance and interpersonal characteristics in college students' romantic relationships. *Personal Relationships, 4,* 25-34.

Van Lange, P. A. M., Rusbult, C. E., Drigotas, S. M., Arriaga, X. B., Witcher, B. S., & Cox, C. L.(1997). Willingness to sacrifice in close relationships. *Journal of Personality and Social Psychology, 72,* 1373-1395.

Vogel, D. L., & Karney, B. R. (2002). Demands and withdraws in newlyweds. *Journal of Social and Personal Relationships, 19,* 685-701.

Vogl-Bauer, S. (2003). Maintaining family relationships. In M. Dainton & D. Canary (Eds.),*Maintaining relationships through communication* (pp. 31-49). Mahwah, NJ: Lawrence Erlbaum.

Waggenspack, B. M., & Hensley, W. E. (1989). Perception of the argumentativeness trait in interpersonal relationship situations. *Social Behavior and Personality, 17,* 111-120.

Waite, L. J., & Gallagher, M. (2000). *The case for marriage: Why married people are happier,healthier, and better off financially.* NY: Doubleday.

Waldinger, R. J., Schulz, M. S., Hauser, S. T., Allen, J. P., & Crowell, J. A. (2004). Reading others' emotions: The role of intuitive judgments in predicting marital satisfaction, quality, and stability. *Journal of Family Psychology, 18,* 58-71.

Wallerstein, J. S., & Blakeslee, S. (1995). *The good marriage: How and why love lasts.* NY:Houghton Mifflin Publishers.

Waring, E. M., Tillman, M. P., Frelick, L., Russell, L., & Weisz, G. (1980). Concepts of intimacy in the general population. *Journal of Nervous and Mental Disease, 168,* 471-474.

Weaver, J. B., Masland, J. L., & Zillman, D. (1984). Effect of erotica on young men's aesthetic perception of their female sexual partners. *Perceptual and Motor Skills, 58,* 929-930.

Wegscheider-Cruse, S. (1989). *Another chance.* Palo Alto, CA: Science and Behavior Books.

Weigel, D. J., & Ballard-Reisch, D. S. (2008). Relational maintenance, satisfaction, and commitment in marriage. *Journal of Family Communication, 8,* 212-229.

Welch, K.J. (2010). *Family Life Now.* NY: Allyn and Bacon.

Whitaker, C., & Napier, A. (1988). *The family crucible.* NY: William Morrow Publishers.

Whitehead, B. D., & Popenoe, D. (2001). The state of our unions: Who wants to marry a soulmate? *The National Marriage Project.* New Brunswick, NJ: Rutgers University.

Williams, B.K., Sawyer, S.C., & Wahlstrom, C.M. (2009). *Marriages, Families, and Intimate Relationships. Boston,* MA: Allyn and Bacon.

Williams, R. & Williams, V. (1993). *Anger kills.* NY: Harper Collins.

Wood, J. T. (1995). *Relational communication: Continuity and change in personal relationships.* Belmont, CA: Wadsworth.

Wood, J. T. (1996). She says / he says: Communication, caring, and conflict in heterosexual relationships. In J. T Wood (Ed.), *Gendered relationships* (pp. 149-162). Mountain View,CA: Mayfield Publishers.

Wood, J. T. (1997). *Gendered lives: Communication, gender, and culture* (2nd ed.). Belmont, CA: Wadsworth.

Wood, J. T. (2012). *Interpersonal communication.* Belmont, CA: Wadsworth.

Wood, J.T., & Fixmer-Oraiz, N. (2014). *Gendered Lives.* Boston, MA: Cengage.

Zillman, D., & Bryant, J. (1988a). Effects of prolonged consumption of pornography on family values. *Journal of Family Issues, 9,* 518-544.

Zillman, D., & Bryant, J. (1988b). Pornography's impact on sexual satisfaction. *Journal of Applied Social Psychology, 18,* 438-453.

About the Author

John Buri received his PhD in Psychology from Loyola University in Chicago in 1976. Since that time, Dr. Buri has been at the University of St. Thomas (UST) in Saint Paul, Minnesota, where he is currently a full Professor in the Department of Psychology. He has received numerous local, regional, and national teaching awards, and has published over sixty journal articles and research papers. Dr. Buri and his wife Kathy have been married for over forty years and they have six children and ten grandchildren.

CPSIA information can be obtained
at www.ICGtesting.com
Printed in the USA
LVHW022149230120
644554LV00005B/111

9 781948 282161